God's Promises Fulfilled

A Scriptural Journey with Jesus the Messiah

Jeanne Kun

the WORD
among us®
Press

The Word Among Us
9639 Doctor Perry Road
Ijamsville, Maryland 21754
www.wordamongus.org
ISBN:978-1-59325-066-9

11 10 09 08 07   2 3 4 5 6

Nihil obstat: The Reverend Michael Morgan, Chancellor
                  Censor Librorum
                  November 18, 2005

Imprimatur: +Most Reverend Victor Galeone
                  Bishop of St. Augustine
                  November 18, 2005

Cover and Book Design: David Crosson

Cover Image: Tito, Santi di (1536-1603) *Entry into Jerusalem*
Location: Accademia, Florence, Italy Photo Credit: Alinari / Art Resource, NY

Made and printed in the United States of America.

Library of Congress Cataloging-in-Publication Data

Kun, Jeanne, 1951-
  God's promises fulfilled : a Scriptural journey with Jesus the Messiah / Jeanne Kun.
     p. cm.
  Includes bibliographical references.
  ISBN 978-1-59325-066-9 (alk. paper)
  1. Messiah--Biblical teaching. 2. Messiah--Prophecies. 3. God--Promises. 4. Jesus Christ--Messiahship. 5. Bible--Criticism, interpretation, etc. I. Title.

BS680.M4L67 1995
232'.1--dc22

2005027669

Contents

Introduction

In the beginning God "spoke" the world into being through the power of his creative word. Then he created Adam and Eve in his own image and initiated a conversation with them in the garden of Eden, revealing himself to them so that they might know, love, and obey him. Even when they were disobedient, God didn't end the dialogue with them. Rather, he mysteriously promised to send one who would trample Satan underfoot and defeat evil, releasing humankind from the consequences of their sin.

The conversation God began with Adam and Eve continued through the centuries with his chosen people, Israel. Time and time again through Israel's prophets he renewed his promise to redeem and restore his people. In enigmatic ways the prophets spoke of God's "anointed one," of a glorious descendant of David who would occupy the throne forever, of a "son of man" whose reign would be everlasting, even of a suffering servant of God. Generation after generation, God's people longed for the coming of this mysterious messenger, even as they wondered just what these prophetic words meant.

In the Fullness of Time

Finally God's conversation with humankind took a radical new turn: "When the time had fully come, God sent forth his Son, born of woman" (Galatians 4:4). God's word became incarnate, the Son of God became man—and in him all the promises of God were fulfilled.

God's Promises Fulfilled: A Scriptural Journey with Jesus the Messiah explores how God "in many and various ways . . . spoke of old to our fathers by the prophets" and also shows how "in these last days he has spoken to us by a Son" (Hebrews 1:1-2). The first three chapters focus our attention on texts from the Old Testament that unfold the promises of God—promises to redeem fallen humankind from sin; to establish his anointed one on the throne of David forever; and to bring an eternal reign of peace and justice. The remaining chapters present gospel scenes that portray Jesus in his messianic role—God's promises fulfilled through the birth, ministry, death, and resurrection of his Son.

The prophecies of the Old Testament form the foundation of our understanding of Jesus the Messiah as he is revealed to us in the New Testament. Familiarity with the promises that God proclaimed through Nathan, Isaiah, Jeremiah, Zephaniah, and other ancient prophets of Israel enhances our appreciation of the fullness of God's word spoken in Jesus, the Word-made-flesh, the Messiah.

The gospels record the words and actions of Jesus, who brought to its climax the conversation that God began with Adam and Eve in the garden. Jesus himself not only declared who he was—the Messiah, the Son of the living God—but what that meant. He proclaimed the reign of God that he had come to establish (Mark 1:14-15) and explained its nature (Matthew 13:44-45; 18:3; Luke 13:20-21; 17:20-21). He rejected the crowd's attempt to make him an earthly king (John 6:15) and stated that his kingdom and kingship were not of this world (18:36). He even announced his impending passion, death, and resurrection to his uncomprehending disciples (Mark 10:32-34). Finally, Jesus was crucified—and the full and ultimate meaning of his messianic identity and role was revealed in the power and the pain of the cross.

After his crucifixion and resurrection, Jesus continued to explain how he fulfilled God's promises and prophetic revelations about the coming of the Messiah. To the two disciples on the road to Emmaus, he put the question, "Was it not necessary that the Christ should suffer these things and enter into his glory?" (Luke 24:26). Then, Luke tells us, "Beginning with Moses and all the prophets, he interpreted to them in all the scriptures the things concerning himself" (24:27). As we proceed through the ten reflections in this book, we too are like the travelers on the road to Emmaus, on a journey through the Scriptures with Jesus the Messiah.

How to Use This Book

The format of God's Promises Fulfilled: A Scriptural Journey with Jesus the Messiah is suited to personal reflection and individual study as well as group discussion. In either case, we suggest that you begin each session with prayer, asking God to speak to you through his word. Although each chapter's Scripture scene is provided in full in this book (in the Catholic edition of the Revised Standard Version), you will find it helpful to have a Bible on hand for looking up other passages and cross-references. Take the time to read carefully and meditate on these Scripture passages, and then read the accompanying section "Reflecting on the Word" to deepen your understanding of the texts.

Two sets of questions are included in each chapter to help you explore the full scope of the passage and consider its relevance to your own life. Those under the heading "Pondering the Word" require an attentive reading of the Scripture selection and focus on the content and meaning of the text. "Living the Word" questions prompt you to apply the lessons and truths learned through Scripture to your own life. Remember, questions allow for a variety of answers and are provided to help you explore the text and its meaning for your life. Be confident that the Spirit will guide you!

"Rooted in the Word" offers brief comments on various attributes of Jesus that are modeled in the corresponding scene. Additional Scripture texts further illustrate the virtue or character trait highlighted in this section. A selection from a Catholic writer—ancient or modern—concludes each chapter. These excerpts, under the heading "Treasuring the Word," are indeed treasures from the church's rich heritage.

If you use this book for personal study or as an aid in your prayer time, read at your own pace—take as much time as you need to meditate on the material and pursue any thoughts it brings to mind. You will gain the most benefit from your study by writing down your answers to the questions in the spaces provided. End your reading or study with a prayer of thanksgiving to God for what you have learned, and ask the Holy Spirit how to apply it to your life.

If you use this book in a Bible-study group, it is especially important that each member take the time to prepare for each session. Read the material decided upon in advance and consider your answers to the questions, so that the group can have a rewarding discussion in the time allotted.

Actively contribute to the discussion, but also listen attentively to the others in the group. Respect the other members of the group and their contributions to the discussion. The group might also want to include a time of prayer during the meetings and designate a leader or moderator to facilitate the discussion.

Welcome Jesus the Messiah more deeply into your life as you encounter him through the pages of this book. The privilege of knowing Jesus brings with it the privilege and blessing of responding to him in personal friendship and discipleship. We pray that each of you will take those steps joyfully as you go forward on your own journey with Jesus the Messiah.

Jeanne Kun
The Word Among Us Press

Paradise Lost

I will put enmity between
     you and the woman,
   and between your seed
       and her seed;
he shall bruise your head,
     and you shall bruise his heel.

Genesis 3:15

By turning from God, Adam and
Eve lost authority over their own
lives, they broke their intimacy with
each other, and they lost union with
God. . . . Who can deliver us from
this incessant twisting of human
relationships?

Francis Martin, *The Fire in the Cloud*

Exiled from Eden

Exiled from Eden
for her transgression,
how Eve must have longed
to make bold and storm its gates
to gain entry once again
(futile though she knew such assault would be)
but dared not.

Instead
you satisfied death's claim
(just punishment for sin)
on Eve and her descendants.
Trespassing in that dark domain,
you strode as conqueror there
to release all death's hostages,
having paid the ransom
(mine, too, along with Eve's)
with your own blood.

And now the cherub
has forever sheathed the flaming sword
that so long barred Eve's way back to Paradise.

[1]Now the serpent was more subtle than any other wild creature that the LORD God had made. He said to the woman, "Did God say, 'You shall not eat of any tree of the garden'?" [2]And the woman said to the serpent, "We may eat of the fruit of the trees of the garden; [3]but God said, 'You shall not eat of the fruit of the tree which is in the midst of the garden, neither shall you touch it, lest you die.'" [4]But the serpent said to the woman, "You will not die. [5]For God knows that when you eat of it your eyes will be opened, and you will be like God, knowing good and evil." [6]So when the woman saw that the tree was good for food, and that it was a delight to the eyes, and that the tree was to be desired to make one wise, she took of its fruit and ate; and she also gave some to her husband, and he ate. [7]Then the eyes of both were opened, and they knew that they were naked; and they sewed fig leaves together and made themselves aprons.

[8]And they heard the sound of the LORD God walking in the garden in the cool of the day, and the man and his wife hid themselves from the presence of the LORD God among the trees of the garden. [9]But the LORD God called to the man, and said to him, "Where are you?" [10]And he said, "I heard the sound of thee in the garden, and I was afraid, because I was naked; and I hid myself." [11]He said, "Who told you that you were naked? Have you eaten of the tree of which I commanded you not to eat?" [12]The man said, "The woman whom thou gavest to be with me, she gave me fruit of the tree, and I ate." [13]Then the LORD God said to the woman, "What is this that you have done?" The woman said, "The serpent beguiled me, and I ate." [14]The LORD God said to the serpent,

"Because you have done this,
    cursed are you above all cattle,
    and above all wild animals;
upon your belly you shall go,
    and dust you shall eat
    all the days of your life.
[15] I will put enmity between
        you and the woman,
    and between your seed
        and her seed;
he shall bruise your head,
    and you shall bruise his heel."

[22]Then the LORD God said, "Behold, the man has become like one of us, knowing good and evil; and now, lest he put forth his hand and take also of the tree of life, and eat, and live for ever"—[23]therefore the LORD God sent him forth from the garden of Eden, to till the ground from which he was taken. [24]He drove out the man; and at the east of the garden of Eden he placed the cherubim, and a flaming sword which turned every way, to guard the way to the tree of life.

Reflecting on the Word

God created the human race to enjoy fellowship with him. His loving design for humankind was that men and women would live in communion with their Creator—an unbroken relationship characterized by the innocence and intimacy of life in the garden of Eden, where God walked "in the cool of the day" amid his creation (Genesis 3:8). Tragically, friendship with God was shattered and innocence was lost when Adam and Eve betrayed this communion. In doing so, they distorted their nature, which had been made in the very image and likeness of God (1:26-27).

Separation from God, sickness, suffering, and death were brought about by Adam and Eve's sin, which also resulted in their banishment from Eden (Genesis 3:23-24). The evil that we see in the world around us—and in our own hearts—is not a part of God's plan for his creation. It stems from the fact that our first parents turned away from God. The consequences were fatal: Every human being is now born into a fallen and fragmented world, a world that has been infected by sin and alienated from God. Our human nature was wounded and weakened by Adam and Eve's sin, so we too incline toward sin and evil.

What was the sin of our first parents? "You may eat freely of every tree of the garden," God told Adam when he placed him as caretaker over Eden, "but of the tree of the knowledge of good and evil you shall not eat" (Genesis 2:16-17). Adam was to trust God and obey his command not out of servile fear, but out of gratitude to the One who had created him in love. "It is the headiest exercise of our liberty to be free to obey," noted Poor Clare abbess Mother Mary Francis. "Adam was lord of the world when he was free to obey. When he surrendered that glorious freedom in order to disobey, . . . well, which human heart does not keep the record of his sorry loss?"

Misusing their freedom, Adam and Eve disobeyed the sole prohibition God had placed on them and ate the mysterious fruit. (Notice that Genesis does not tell of an apple, though that is what we popularly visualize Eve reaching for!) By this act, they were asserting themselves against the moral limits God had established for them as his creatures and were, in a sense, usurping the place of God. As the *Catechism of the Catholic Church* states:

> Man, tempted by the devil, let his trust in his Creator die in his heart and, abusing his freedom, disobeyed God's command. This is what man's first sin consisted of. All subsequent sin would be disobedience toward God and lack of trust in his goodness.
>
> In that sin man *preferred* himself to God and by that very act scorned him. He chose himself over and against God, against the requirements of his creaturely status and therefore against his own good. (CCC, 397–398)

In the libretto of composer Franz Joseph Haydn's famous oratorio, *The Creation*, we are offered another insight into the nature of Adam and Eve's sin. Meant to be forever happy, they were "misled by false conceit" and exercised their free will *against* God instead of toward him. Not content with what had been given them, they desired what was forbidden: "Ye strive at more [than] granted is, and more desire to know, [than] know ye should."

What about the serpent? "Behind the disobedient choice of our first parents lurks a seductive voice, opposed to God, which makes them fall into death out of envy [Genesis 3:1-5, Wisdom 2:24]" (CCC, 391). Scripture and the church's tradition recognize in the deceitful snake a fallen angel, called "Satan" or the "devil." According to the teaching of the church, Satan and the other demons were created by God to be good, but of their own free will chose evil. In Eden, the serpent led Eve into sin by insinuating that God was jealously withholding from her and Adam something that would give them independence and power: "God knows that when you eat of it your eyes will be opened, and you will be like God, knowing good and evil" (Genesis 3:5). Recalling the deadly role played in Genesis by the cunning serpent, we commonly depict Satan as a snake. And in Revelation 20:2, we read of the binding of "the dragon, that ancient serpent, who is the Devil and Satan."

By their sin, Adam and Eve lost their union with God as well as intimacy with one another. Ashamed of their disobedience and nakedness, they feared God and hid themselves from him. Yet God sought them out (Genesis 3:8-9). Because he loved this man and woman whom he had created in his image to enjoy communion with him, he was not about to let his plan for them—and for the entire human race—be foiled. Even as Adam and Eve tried to disclaim their fault and shift blame from themselves (3:12-13), God promised to reverse the consequences of sin and to triumph over evil. Addressing the serpent, he said,

> I will put enmity between you and
> the woman,
> and between your seed and her
> seed;
> he shall bruise your head,
> and you shall bruise his heel.
> (3:15)

This verse gives a mysterious hint of redemption for humankind, foretelling a conflict in which evil would be trampled underfoot by the offspring of the woman. The Fathers of the Church later recognized in it a reference to Jesus and a veiled prophecy of the victory of Christ over Satan. Genesis 3:15 is called the "Proto-Gospel," because it is the first announcement to Adam and Eve—and in them, to the entire human race in need of redemption—of the Messiah-Redeemer.

In the New Testament, Luke's genealogy calls Jesus "the son of Adam, the son of God" (Luke 3:38), and St. Paul saw in Jesus a new Adam (see Romans 5:14, 17; 1 Corinthians 15:21-22, 45). One of the first ways the church characterized the Virgin Mary, the mother of the promised Savior, is as the new Eve. As St. Irenaeus noted,

As Eve was seduced by the word of an angel and so fled from God after disobeying his word, Mary in her turn was given the good news by the word of an angel, and bore God in obedience to his word. As Eve was seduced into disobedience to God, so Mary was persuaded into obedience to God; thus the Virgin Mary became the advocate of the virgin Eve. (*Against Heresies*)

The ease with which Adam and Eve succumbed to Satan's temptation in the garden stands in sharp contrast to the determination with which Jesus would later reject Satan's allurements in the wilderness (Matthew 4:1-11). And Christ's obedience to his Father would redeem humankind from the effects of Adam's disobedience: "For as by one man's disobedience many were made sinners, so by one man's obedience many will be made righteous" (Romans 5:19).

With Adam and Eve's fall, the stage was set for divine intervention into human history. We are reminded of this irony in the *Exsultet* sung during the Easter Vigil liturgy: "O happy fault, O necessary sin of Adam, which gained for us so great a Redeemer!" This first sin, devastating and abhorrent as it was, was the prelude to the coming of the Savior to redeem humankind and renew our fellowship with God.

This promise of Genesis 3:15 would be fulfilled through Jesus Christ, born of Mary. Yet humankind was to wait outside Eden's closed gates for many generations before Jesus would restore our relationship with the Father and open the kingdom of heaven to us. The Old Testament is a record of the unfolding of God's promises as his people yearned for that salvation to be made manifest in the coming of the Messiah.

Pondering the Word

1. What do you think "the tree of the knowledge of good and evil" (Genesis 2:9) symbolized? How would you interpret the expression "knowing good and evil" (3:5)?

_____

_____

_____

_____

_____

_____

_____

_____

_____

2. Why might God have prohibited Adam and Eve from eating of the tree of the knowledge of good and evil (Genesis 2:17)?

_____

_____

_____

_____

_____

_____

_____

_____

3. Describe the serpents' tactics for leading Eve into disobedience (Genesis 3:1-5). Note the progressive stages of the serpent's conversation with her. What does this indicate to you about Satan and the nature of evil?

_____

_____

_____

_____

_____

_____

_____

_____

_____

4. What were the immediate consequences of Adam and Eve's disobedience? The long-term consequences?

_____

_____

_____

_____

_____

_____

_____

_____

_____

5. What was the purpose of God's conversation with Adam and Eve (Genesis 3:9-13), since he already knew that they had disobeyed him? What does this conversation suggest to you about Adam and Eve's relationship with God? With one another as husband and wife?

_____

_____

_____

_____

_____

_____

_____

_____

_____

_____

6. Why do you think God expelled Adam and Eve from Eden? God's words to the serpent seem to give them a promise of hope (Genesis 3:14-15). What does this reveal about God's heart toward his creation after Adam and Eve had disobeyed him?

_____

_____

_____

_____

_____

_____

_____

_____

_____

_____

Living the Word

1. Why do you think God desired to create humankind in his image and likeness (Genesis 1:26-27)? In what ways do you think human beings share God's image? How do you see the image and likeness of God reflected in others? In yourself?

_____

_____

_____

_____

_____

_____

_____

_____

_____

_____

2. What consequences of sin—your own and that of others—do you recognize in your life? In society at large?

_____

_____

_____

_____

_____

_____

_____

_____

_____

_____

3. Have you ever attempted to justify your sins? What excuses do you make? How can you take personal responsibility for your failings and avoid placing blame for your own sins elsewhere?

_____

_____

_____

_____

_____

_____

_____

_____

_____

_____

4. Adam and Eve hid from God after they sinned. Are there any ways in which you are hiding from God? If so, why?

_____

_____

_____

_____

_____

_____

_____

_____

_____

_____

5. In what ways have you personally encountered evil and the deceptions of Satan? How do you resist and combat temptations to sin? What can you do to protect yourself against attacks of Satan and the influence of evil?

_____

_____

_____

_____

_____

_____

_____

_____

_____

_____

6. Imagine Adam and Eve's existence in Eden before they were estranged from God. What aspects of this state appeal to you the most? How does this reflect your image of spending eternity with God?

_____

_____

_____

_____

_____

_____

_____

_____

_____

_____

Rooted in the Word

Jesus: A Portrait of Obedience to the Father

Beguiled by Satan's lies, Adam and Eve fell into his trap and disobeyed God's command. As a consequence of their fall, sin came into the world through them—"and so death spread to all men because all men sinned" (Romans 5:12). Adam and Eve—whose name means "the mother of all living" (Genesis 3:20)—are called the parents of the human race, yet ironically they also brought death to it. Through sin, human beings suffered more than merely a physical death, but also a spiritual death—separation from God and the impossibility of everlasting life with him.

If by Adam and Eve's defeat humankind fell into the bondage of death, so by another human's victory—that of the Word-made-flesh in Jesus—we rise again to life. By Jesus' total submission to the Father, even to death, the human race was redeemed; our relationship to the Father was restored, and we are able to share again in eternal life: "Then as one man's trespass led to condemnation for all men, so one man's act of righteousness leads to acquittal and life for all men" (Romans 5:18).

In his cycle of poems about God's plan of salvation and his Son's incarnation, St. John of the Cross imagines a conversation in which Jesus expresses his obedience to his Father's will to rescue us from eternal death:

My will is yours, the Son replied,
dear Father, and my glory is
that your will should be always mine;
no greater joy to me than this.

And I find it fitting, Father,
what you, the All-highest, say,
for your goodness and your mercy
are more visible this way. . . .

I will go seeking my own Bride,
taking upon myself the care,
the weariness, the labours she
has borne in her long waiting there.

And so that she, my Love, may live,
for her dear sake I'll gladly die,
drawing her back from that deep place
I'll bring her safe to you on high.

Read and prayerfully reflect on these additional Scripture passages that describe how Jesus acted in trusting obedience to God:

Then I said, "Lo, I come;
   in the roll of the book it is
     written of me;
I delight to do thy will,
   O my God;
   thy law is within my heart."
(Psalm 40:7-8)

[Jesus] fell on his face and prayed, "My Father, if it be possible, let this cup pass from me; nevertheless, not as I will, but as thou wilt." (Matthew 26:39)

[Jesus said to his disciples:] "I have come down from heaven, not to do my own will, but the will of him who sent me; and this is the will of him who sent me, that I should lose nothing of all that he has given me, but raise it up at the last day." (John 6:38-39)

[Jesus said:] "For this reason the Father loves me, because I lay down my life, that I may take it again. No one takes it from me, but I lay it down of my own accord. I have power to lay it down, and I have power to take it again; this charge I have received from my Father." (John 10:17-18)

Being found in human form [Jesus] humbled himself and became obedient unto death, even death on a cross. (Philippians 2:8)

A Reading from First Vespers as Sung in the Eastern Orthodox Church on the Sunday before Lent

The Casting Out of Adam from Paradise

The Lord my Creator took me as dust from the earth and formed me into a living creature, breathing into me the breath of life and giving me a soul; He honoured me, setting me as ruler upon earth over all things visible, and making me companion of the angels. But Satan the deceiver, using the serpent as his instrument, enticed me by food; he parted me from the glory of God and gave me over to the earth and to the lowest depths of death. But, Master, in compassion call me back again.

In my wretchedness I have cast off the robe woven by God, disobeying Thy divine command, O Lord, at the counsel of the enemy; and I am clothed now in fig leaves and in garments of skin. I am condemned to eat the bread of oil in the sweat of my brow, and the earth has been cursed so that it bears thorns and thistles for me. But, Lord, who in the last times wast made flesh of a Virgin, call me back again and bring me into Paradise.

O precious Paradise, unsurpassed in beauty, tabernacle built by God, unending gladness and delight, glory of righteousness, joy of the prophets, and dwelling of the saints, with the sound of thy leaves pray to the Maker of all: may He open unto me the gates which I closed by my transgression, and may He count me worthy to partake of the Tree of Life and of the joy which was mine when I dwelt in thee before. . . .

Adam sat before Paradise and, lamenting his nakedness, he wept: 'Woe is me! By evil deceit was I persuaded and led astray, and now I am an exile from glory. Woe is me! In my simplicity I was stripped naked, and now I am in want. O Paradise, no more shall I take pleasure in thy joy; no more shall I look upon the Lord my God and Maker, for I shall return to the earth whence I was taken. O merciful and compassionate Lord, to Thee I cry aloud: I am fallen, have mercy upon me.'

The sun hid its rays, the moon and stars were turned to blood, the mountains were afraid, the hills trembled, when Paradise was shut. Adam departed, beating his hands upon his face and saying: 'I am fallen: merciful Lord, have mercy on me.'. . .

Adam was cast out of Paradise through eating from the tree. Seated before the gates he wept, lamenting with a pitiful voice and saying: 'Woe is me, what I have suffered in my misery! I transgressed one commandment of the Master, and now I am deprived of every blessing. O most holy Paradise, planted for my sake and shut because of Eve, pray to Him that made thee and fashioned me, that once more I may take pleasure in thy flowers.' Then the Saviour said to him: 'I desire not the loss of the creature which I fashioned, but that he should be saved and come to knowledge of the truth [1 Timothy 2:4]; and when he comes to me I will not cast him out' [John 6:37]. . . .

Theotokion

Christ the Lord, my Maker and Redeemer, came forth from thy womb, all-hallowed Queen, and clothing Himself in me He delivered Adam from the curse of old. Therefore with never-silent voices we praise thee as true Mother of God and Virgin, and with the salutation of the Angel we cry unto thee: Hail, Lady, guardian and protection and salvation of our souls.

The House of David

Your house and your kingdom shall be made sure for ever before me; your throne shall be established for ever.

2 Samuel 7:16

It is the Son of the Most High alone who is the key of David that shuts and no man opens, and in whom are hidden all the treasures of wisdom and of knowledge.

St. Bernard of Clairvaux,
In Adventu Domini I, 1-10

Of Shepherds and Kings

As young David, Jesse's son,
herded sheep in the rock-strewn fields
near Bethlehem (city of his birth)
little did he dream
he'd be king one day
and shepherd of God's people Israel.

And still less did lowly herdsmen
later dream they'd see
great David's greater son
lying in a manger,
and bright angelic hosts above those same fields
heralding this strange, glad news
as they watched o'er their flocks.

The baby born in Bethlehem
sleeps now quietly upon the straw
(no golden cradle for this humble heir of royal David).
Perhaps he's dreaming of the day
he'll gather his sheep to himself
(there shall be one flock, one shepherd then)
and none shall snatch them from his hand.

2 Samuel 7:1-22, 28-29
The Scene

¹Now when the king [David] dwelt in his house, and the LORD had given him rest from all his enemies round about, ²the king said to Nathan the prophet, "See now, I dwell in a house of cedar, but the ark of God dwells in a tent." ³And Nathan said to the king, "Go, do all that is in your heart; for the LORD is with you."

⁴But that same night the word of the LORD came to Nathan, ⁵"Go and tell my servant David, 'Thus says the LORD: Would you build me a house to dwell in? ⁶I have not dwelt in a house since the day I brought up the people of Israel from Egypt to this day, but I have been moving about in a tent for my dwelling. ⁷In all places where I have moved with all the people of Israel, did I speak a word with any of the judges of Israel, whom I commanded to shepherd my people Israel, saying, "Why have you not built me a house of cedar?"' ⁸Now therefore thus you shall say to my servant David, 'Thus says the LORD of hosts, I took you from the pasture, from following the sheep, that you should be prince over my people Israel; ⁹and I have been with you wherever you went, and have cut off all your enemies from before you; and I will make for you a great name, like the name of the great ones of the earth. ¹⁰And I will appoint a place for my people Israel, and will plant them, that they may dwell in their own place, and be disturbed no more; and violent men shall afflict them no more, as formerly, ¹¹from the time that I appointed judges over my people Israel; and I will give you rest from all your enemies. Moreover the LORD declares to you that the LORD will make you a house. ¹²When your days are fulfilled and you lie down with your fathers, I will raise up your offspring after you, who shall come forth from your body, and I will establish his kingdom. ¹³He shall build a house for my name, and I will establish the throne of his kingdom for ever. ¹⁴I will be his father, and he shall be my son. When he commits iniquity, I will chasten him with the rod of men, with the stripes of the sons of men; ¹⁵but I will not take my steadfast love from him, as I took it from Saul, whom I put away from before you. ¹⁶And your house and your kingdom shall be made sure for ever before me; your throne shall be established for ever.'" ¹⁷In accordance with all these words, and in accordance with all this vision, Nathan spoke to David.

¹⁸Then King David went in and sat before the LORD, and said, "Who am I, O Lord GOD, and what is my house, that thou hast brought me thus far? ¹⁹And yet this was a small thing in thy eyes, O Lord GOD; thou hast spoken also of thy servant's house for a great while to come, and hast shown me future generations, O Lord GOD! ²⁰And what more can David say to thee? For thou knowest thy servant, O Lord GOD! ²¹Because of thy promise, and according to thy own heart, thou hast wrought all this greatness, to make thy servant know it. ²²Therefore thou art great, O LORD God; for there is none like thee, and there is no

God besides thee, according to all that we have heard with our ears. . . . [28]And now, O Lord God, thou art God, and thy words are true, and thou hast promised this good thing to thy servant; [29]now therefore may it please thee to bless the house of thy servant, that it may continue for ever before thee; for thou, O Lord God, hast spoken, and with thy blessing shall the house of thy servant be blessed for ever."

Psalm 89:19-21, 27-37

[19] Of old thou didst speak in a vision
    to thy faithful one, and say:
  "I have set the crown upon one who
    is mighty,
  I have exalted one chosen from
    the people.
[20] I have found David, my servant;
    with my holy oil I have anointed
    him;
[21] so that my hand shall ever abide
    with him,
    my arm also shall strengthen him.

[27] And I will make him the first-born,
    the highest of the kings of the earth.
[28] My steadfast love I will keep for him
    for ever,
    and my covenant will stand firm
    for him.
[29] I will establish his line for ever
    and his throne as the days of the
    heavens.
[30] If his children forsake my law
    and do not walk according to my
    ordinances,
[31] if they violate my statutes
    and do not keep my commandments,
[32] then I will punish their transgression
    with the rod
    and their iniquity with scourges;
[33] but I will not remove from him my
    steadfast love,
    or be false to my faithfulness.
[34] I will not violate my covenant,
    or alter the word that went forth
    from my lips.
[35] Once for all I have sworn by my
    holiness;
    I will not lie to David.
[36] His line shall endure for ever,
    his throne as long as the sun
    before me.
[37] Like the moon it shall be established
    for ever;
    it shall stand firm while the skies
    endure."

Reflecting on the Word

Before God sent Adam and Eve out of the garden of Eden, he intimated that evil would ultimately be defeated by the seed of the woman (Genesis 3:15). This was the first hint of how God would restore humankind to full union with him. True to his promise, over time he revealed his plan of salvation to the people he called his own.

First the Lord made a covenant with the patriarch Abraham and promised to make him the father of a nation through whom all the earth would be blessed (Genesis 12:2-3; 15:7-12, 17-21; 17:1-8). This promise extended beyond Abraham to his offspring "throughout their generations for an everlasting covenant" (17:7).

When Abraham's descendants had become slaves in Egypt, God delivered them. Then he made a covenant on Sinai with Moses and the Israelites, bringing them into a special relationship with him as his chosen people (Exodus 19:5-6; 24:7-8). Later, when they asked for a king to rule them, the Lord appointed Saul to the task (1 Samuel 9:15-17; 10:1). After Saul's disobedience (15:1-23), the shepherd David, the youngest son of Jesse, was anointed king over Israel (16:1-13).

Anointing with oil—that is, pouring oil from a horn or vessel on the head of one to be made king—was a symbolic act that consecrated the person to God's service. Priests (Exodus 30:30), prophets (1 Kings 19:16), and even holy objects such as altars, vessels, and lampstands (Exodus 30:26-29) could also be anointed with oil to indicate that they, too, were consecrated to God. "Messiah"—*mashiach* in Hebrew, and *christos* in Greek—literally means the "anointed one," and the title "the Lord's anointed" originally referred to the king who ruled over God's people.

When King David had secured peace within his kingdom and with the surrounding nations (2 Samuel 7:1), he desired to honor God by building a "house" for him in Jerusalem. In the ancient world a god was truly established when he had a fitting home. The temple that David decided to build for the Lord was to replace the tent that had sheltered the Ark of the Covenant since the days at Sinai (7:2, 6); he also intended it to be a place of worship, where praise and sacrifices would be offered to God.

Instead of affirming David's plan, God surprised him by revealing a much grander plan. Through the prophet Nathan, God told King David that he was not to construct a dwelling place for him. Rather, God intended to build a "house" for David, that is, a dynasty that would rule over his people. The Lord declared to David that one of his descendants would always sit on the throne, thus promising to establish David's house for all time: "Your house and your kingdom shall be made sure for ever before me; your throne shall be established for ever" (2 Samuel 7:16). Notice the word play and variety of meanings for the word "house" as God spoke to David through Nathan: palace (7:1), dwelling (7:2, 5, 6, 7), temple (7:13), and royal dynasty (7:11, 16).

This promise to David amplified the covenants with Abraham and with Israel at Sinai. God did not expect or require anything of David in return for the promise; it was a grant made freely to King David and his descendants, not a treaty that stipulated obligations.

Solomon succeeded to his father David's throne, but soon after his death, Israel and Judah, which had been united as one kingdom under David, broke apart. The monarchy was plagued with strife and began to decline under Solomon's son, King Rehoboam, and his heirs. Two centuries later (around 722 B.C.) Israel was vanquished by Assyria, and Judah was made Assyria's vassal. In 587 B.C. the Babylonians wiped out Judah, destroying the temple, burning Jerusalem, and sending many of the city's inhabitants into exile. Yet memories of the brilliant days of David's reign lived on in God's chosen people.

Despite the failings of the kings of Israel, Judah, and his chosen people, God did not retract his promises to them. Instead, he continued to love them steadfastly and to unfold his plan for salvation through the prophets that he sent to them. As Benedictine monk and Scripture scholar Damasus Winzen noted, "Through all the human confusion of defeat and victory, of treachery and loyalty, of disappointments and triumph, we can hear—if we have ears to listen—the quiet steps of God's fatherly love pursuing the path of redemption" (*Pathways in Scripture*).

The Jewish people recalled the promises God had made to King David, promises of an eternal dynasty and of a kingdom that would last forever. Faced with the disasters and sins of the monarchy that unfolded after the reign of David, they came to hope that these promises would be fulfilled by a future "hero-king." This anointed leader or "messiah" would be descended from David, a conqueror who would throw off the oppressor's yoke, restore the kingdom, and establish perfect justice. Jewish expectations were focused on the "David" of the future—a figure who would revive and carry on the glorious reign of David forever.

Many of the Old Testament psalms—among them, Psalms 2, 45, 89, 100, and 110—have royal and messianic overtones. Several are quoted in the New Testament as prophecies about Jesus, who fulfilled Israel's hopes and yearnings for the rule of one who would truly be God's anointed King and Messiah. Psalm 89 in particular recounts God's dealings with Israel and joyously celebrates the absolute and unconditional promise that God made to establish David's dynasty. Although David and his descendants failed to keep God's commands and were to be justly punished as a consequence (Psalm 89:31-33), God nevertheless declared,

I will not violate my covenant,
or alter the word that went forth
from my lips.

Once for all I have sworn by my
    holiness;
    I will not lie to David.
His line shall endure for ever.
(89:34-36)

However, in events that seemed to belie God's word, Israel fell into disgrace at the hands of a foreign nation; her king was brought down, and it appeared that David's line had been cut off (Psalm 89:38-45). How could Israel reconcile this destruction with God's promises? The situation required that God's promise to David be understood in a new sense—as a description of an ideal king who would one day inherit David's throne.

Psalm 89 ends with a great cry wrenched from the heart of a disappointed yet hopeful people (89:46-52). In anguish, the psalmist implores God to remember his promise and restore his people by sending a righteous king to reign over them again:

Lord, where is thy steadfast love
    of old,
    which by thy faithfulness thou
        didst swear to David?
(89:49)

The people of Israel were mistaken in their understanding and expectation of a political ruler, yet their faith would finally be vindicated: God would answer their pleas not by restoring the ancient monarchy but by raising up, in the words of one hymn writer, "great David's greater son." A descendant of David would in the end rule as king over all.

When the prophet Samuel anointed David as king of Israel, the Spirit of God "came mightily" upon him (1 Samuel 16:13). This is a prefiguration of the baptism of Jesus, the "Christ," God's anointed one (Matthew 3:16). The *Jerusalem Catecheses*, a catechetical work of the early church, explains,

Christ bathed in the river Jordan, imparting to its waters the fragrance of his divinity, and when he came up from them the Holy Spirit descended upon him. . . . Christ's anointing was not by human hands, nor was it with ordinary oil. On the contrary, having destined him to be the Savior of the whole world, the Father himself anointed him with the Holy Spirit.

Immediately following his account of Jesus' baptism, John the Evangelist records the first proclamation of Jesus' messianic identity: "[Andrew] first found his brother Simon, and said to him, 'We have found the Messiah' (which means Christ)" (John 1:41). Ultimately, God's promise to David and Israel's hopes would be fulfilled in the person of Jesus Christ.

Pondering the Word

1. List the phrases in Nathan's prophecy that detail specific aspects of God's promises to David. What predominant themes run through these promises?

_____

_____

_____

_____

_____

_____

_____

_____

_____

2. What does God's covenant with David indicate about God's nature and character?

_____

_____

_____

_____

_____

_____

_____

_____

_____

3. Identify the verses in Nathan's prophecy and in the selection from Psalm 89 that express the absolute nature of God's covenant with David and his descendants. Why, in your opinion, did God make his promises unconditional?

_____

_____

_____

_____

_____

_____

_____

_____

_____

_____

4. Read 2 Samuel 7:18-22, 28-29, David's response after he had received God's word through Nathan. What does this prayer suggest about David's relationship with the Lord? About David's character and how he perceived himself?

_____

_____

_____

_____

_____

_____

_____

_____

_____

5. With what titles and attributes is the king described in Psalm 89:19-21, 27-37?

_____

_____

_____

_____

_____

_____

_____

_____

_____

6. Which of God's promises to David were literally fulfilled in him and his descendants? Which would only be fulfilled in Jesus?

_____

_____

_____

_____

_____

_____

_____

_____

_____

Living the Word

1. God chose David, Jesse's youngest son and thus an improbable candidate, to be king. Recall some of the surprising ways in which God has called you to serve him. Do you find it difficult to accept God's right to call you and use you in whatever way he chooses? If so, why?

2. By promising to build a "house" for David—a dynasty that would rule over his people—God blessed David in a way that far exceeded his expectations. How have you seen God bless and honor you in undeserved and unexpected ways?

3. When your experience and circumstances seem to contradict the promises of God, how do you respond? What might you do to grow in a deeper trust in God and a clearer understanding of his word?

_____

_____

_____

_____

_____

_____

_____

_____

_____

4. God used the prophet Nathan to speak to David. Whom has God used to speak his word to you? What impact did this have on you? Have you ever felt called to speak God's word to another person? What happened when you obeyed God?

_____

_____

_____

_____

_____

_____

_____

_____

_____

5. In what ways do you experience Jesus' kingship and authority over your life? How do you express honor for him as your King?

_____

_____

_____

_____

_____

_____

_____

_____

_____

6. Write a prayer to praise God and acknowledge some of the ways that he has shown his faithfulness and steadfast love to you. You may find it helpful to model your prayer on David's (2 Samuel 7:18-22, 28-29).

_____

_____

_____

_____

_____

_____

_____

_____

_____

Jesus: A Portrait of Kingship

Under the old covenant, God commissioned anointed kings to rule over Israel and Judah. David—whose dynasty God promised to establish forever—was Israel's greatest king, the model and prototype for all future kings. Under the new covenant, God commissioned the Lord Jesus, his own Son as well as a descendant of David, as his anointed King. "The time is fulfilled, and the kingdom of God is at hand," Jesus announced as he took up the mission entrusted to him by the Father (Mark 1:15).

We commonly understand a kingdom to be a territory or country ruled by a king. However, when Jesus spoke of the "kingdom of God," he was not referring to a piece of land, but to the rule of God. Thus, the "kingdom" that Jesus proclaimed in the gospels is better understood as the reign or the kingship and authority exercised by God over his people.

Jesus' ministry and deeds reflect the way in which he would rule as King. His teachings help us understand the nature of his kingdom: "Whoever does not receive the kingdom of God like a child shall not enter it" (Mark 10:15); "Blessed are the poor in spirit, for theirs is the kingdom of heaven" (Matthew 5:3). Jesus also unfolded the truths and mysteries of the kingdom through his parables: "The kingdom of heaven is like leaven which a woman took and hid in three measures of meal, till it was all leavened" (Matthew 13:33); "The kingdom of heaven is like treasure hidden in a field" (13:44).

At the end of the ages, Jesus will come again to establish the full reign of God over the human race—and then we will hear "loud voices in heaven, saying, 'The kingdom of the world has become the kingdom of our Lord and of his Christ, and he shall reign for ever and ever'" (Revelation 11:15)!

Read and prayerfully reflect on these additional Scripture passages to enhance your understanding of Jesus' kingship and of the kingdom of God:

My heart overflows with a goodly
theme;
I address my verses to the king;
my tongue is like the pen of a ready
scribe.

You are the fairest of the sons of men;
grace is poured upon your lips;
therefore God has blessed you
for ever.
Gird your sword upon your thigh,
O mighty one,
in your glory and majesty!

In your majesty ride forth victoriously
for the cause of truth and to
defend the right;
let your right hand teach you
dread deeds!
Your arrows are sharp
in the heart of the king's enemies;
the peoples fall under you.

Your divine throne endures for ever
and ever.
Your royal scepter is a scepter of
equity;
you love righteousness and hate
wickedness.
Therefore God, your God, has
anointed you
with the oil of gladness above
your fellows
(Psalm 45:1-7)

These twelve Jesus sent out, charging them, . . . "[P]reach as you go, saying, 'The kingdom of heaven is at hand.' Heal the sick, raise the dead, cleanse lepers, cast out demons." (Matthew 10:5, 7-8)

[Jesus said:] "When the Son of man comes in his glory, and all the angels with him, then he will sit on his glorious throne. Before him will be gathered all the nations, and he will separate them one from another as a shepherd separates the sheep from the goats, and he will place the sheep at his right hand, but the goats at the left. Then the King will say to those at his right hand, 'Come, O blessed of my Father, inherit the kingdom prepared for you from the foundation of the world.'" (Matthew 25:31-34)

[Jesus said:] "With what can we compare the kingdom of God, or what parable shall we use for it? It is like a grain of mustard seed, which, when sown upon the ground, is the smallest of all the seeds on earth; yet when it is sown it grows up and becomes the greatest of all shrubs, and puts forth large branches, so that the birds of the air can make nests in its shade." (Mark 4:30-32)

I [John] heard every creature in heaven and on earth and under the earth and in the sea, and all therein, saying, "To him who sits upon the throne and to the Lamb be blessing and honor and glory and might for ever and ever!" (Revelation 5:13)

Treasuring the Word

A Reading from *Pathways in Scripture* by Damasus Winzen, OSB

David, Prototype of Christ

The youngest among his brothers, David was called from shepherding his father's flock on Bethlehem's fields to be anointed by Samuel. "And the Spirit of the Lord seized upon David from that day forward" (1 Samuel 16:11-13).

. . . David is the figure of the messianic king of whom Isaiah says: "A shoot shall spring from the stump of Jesse [David's father, 1 Samuel 16:1], and a sprout from his root will bear fruit, and the Spirit of the Lord will rest upon him" (Isaiah 11:1). This prophecy found its fulfillment in the Son of David whom the Spirit descended upon as a dove . . . (Matthew 3:17).

There are many other traits in the life of young David which show him to be the prototype of Christ, especially his fight with Goliath (1 Samuel 17). Faith and spirit had left the Israelites and their king Saul. They did not dare to answer the giant's blasphemies. Then David jumped into the breach, without armor, a true soldier of his God, knowing that "not with sword or spear does the Lord deliver, for the battle is the Lord's" (17:47). With a sling, a stone and a stick, David overcomes all the most up-to-date might of Goliath

(17:5). Who would not be reminded of Christ, the one who jumped into the breach to give his life for the whole people and conquered the power of Satan with the cross on his shoulder?

Another beautiful sign of the love of Christ prefigured in the life of young David is the friendship between him and Jonathan (1 Samuel, chapters 18–20). Jonathan, who as a son of Saul was heir to the kingdom, prefers to be excommunicated by his father rather than to give up David, "whom he loved as his own life" (18:3). He takes off his royal cloak, his sword, his bow and his girdle and gives them to David. By this act he renounces his natural right to the throne in favor of David. He entrusts his own life and that of his family completely to the good graces of his friend: "O may you, if I am still alive, O may you show me the kindness of the Lord!" (20:14). In doing this he represents that portion of Israel which at the time of Christ will prefer to be banned by their own people rather than leave the Son of David, who through his incarnation had received the royal garment of Israel. It was this Jonathan-group among the Jews, the apostles, to whom Christ revealed the secret of his friendship: "Greater love than this no man has, that a man lay down his life for his friends. You are my friends" (John 15:13-14). The friendship between David and Jonathan was fulfilled in Christ who did more for his friends than David ever did. He laid down his life for them.

David's friendship with Jonathan marks the beginning of those long years of trial which make him still more a figure of Christ (1 Samuel, chapters 21–29). The desert becomes David's refuge. Abandoned by all, without arms, without food, he receives from the priest the holy bread of the Lord, which was always kept in the sanctuary (21:3-6), and the sword of Goliath which also had been preserved in the tabernacle. At every turn God shows that David is his anointed one, the man according to his heart. David himself could not have given better witness to the love of God working in his heart than he did by answering Saul's incessant persecution by sparing his life (24:6; 26:9). . . .

David himself was the "Christ," the "anointed one" of the Lord (Psalm 132:17). His name—David, the beloved one (see Matthew 3:17)—his birthplace Bethlehem

(see Luke 2:11), his youth as a shepherd (1 Samuel 17:34-37), his beauty (16:12): really everything in his life foreshadows the Messiah. He won the hearts of his fellow-countrymen through his kindness, and the bond thus established between him and his people points to the new covenant of love between Christ and his Church. Indeed, what the tribes of Israel said to David the day he was proclaimed their king: "We are bones of your bones and flesh of your flesh" (2 Samuel 5:1), gives us the first inkling of the great mystery of the mystical body of Christ which St. Paul was later to reveal. David's wars and victories have also a messianic character. "It is God that girds me with strength, that teaches my hands to war" (Psalm 18:32, 34). It is God that lights David's candle in darkness, by whom he leaps over the wall (Psalm 18:28-29). His victories are anticipations of the great victory which the "Son of David" won at his resurrection. The "sure mercies of David" of which Isaiah speaks (55:3) are fulfilled in Jesus, the Son of David, who did not see corruption, because God raised him from the dead (Acts 13:34-37).

Isaiah's Oracles of Hope

There shall come forth a shoot
from the stump of Jesse,
and a branch shall grow
out of his roots.

Isaiah 11:1

O Flower of Jesse's stem, you
have been raised up as a sign for
all peoples; kings stand silent in
your presence; the nations bow
down in worship before you.
Come, let nothing keep you from
coming to our aid.

Advent Antiphon,
The Liturgy of the Hours

Hope Revived

There shall come forth a shoot from the stump of Jesse,
and a branch shall grow out of his roots.

Come, O Lord,
and in my heart
oft times as dry as Jesse's stump
and broken like that felled tree of David,
take root again.
In a springtime miracle,
blossom forth in me
with the green and bursting vigor of new life.

And the Spirit of the LORD *shall rest upon him.*

Come, O Lord,
in the force and freshness of your Spirit
and blow over me.
Wake in me all that has grown weary
and rouse all that has been dulled by griefs and sorrow.
Refresh and quicken me;
let me find my breath in you
and draw new strength from your vitality.

2 The people who walked in darkness
    have seen a great light;
those who dwelt in a land of deep
    darkness,
    on them has light shined.

3 Thou hast multiplied the nation,
    thou hast increased its joy;
they rejoice before thee
    as with joy at the harvest,
    as men rejoice when they divide
    the spoil.

4 For the yoke of his burden,
    and the staff for his shoulder,
    the rod of his oppressor,
    thou hast broken as on the day of
    Midian.

5 For every boot of the tramping warrior
    in battle tumult
    and every garment rolled in blood
    will be burned as fuel for the fire.

6 For to us a child is born,
    to us a son is given;
and the government will be upon his
    shoulder,
    and his name will be called
"Wonderful Counselor, Mighty God,
    Everlasting Father, Prince of
    Peace."

7 Of the increase of his government
    and of peace
    there will be no end,
upon the throne of David, and over
    his kingdom,
    to establish it, and to uphold it
with justice and with righteousness
    from this time forth and for
    evermore.
The zeal of the LORD of hosts will
    do this.

See also Isaiah 7:1-17

Isaiah 11:1-9 The Scene

1 There shall come forth a shoot from
    the stump of Jesse,
  and a branch shall grow out of his
    roots.
2 And the Spirit of the LORD shall rest
    upon him,
  the spirit of wisdom and
    understanding,
  the spirit of counsel and might,
  the spirit of knowledge and the fear
    of the LORD.
3 And his delight shall be in the fear of
    the LORD.

  He shall not judge by what his
    eyes see,
  or decide by what his ears hear;
4 but with righteousness he shall
    judge the poor,
  and decide with equity for the
    meek of the earth;
  and he shall smite the earth with
    the rod of his mouth,
  and with the breath of his lips
    he shall slay the wicked.

5 Righteousness shall be the girdle
    of his waist,
  and faithfulness the girdle of
    his loins.

6 The wolf shall dwell with the lamb,
  and the leopard shall lie down
    with the kid,
  and the calf and the lion and the
    fatling together,
  and a little child shall lead them.
7 The cow and the bear shall feed;
  their young shall lie down
    together;
  and the lion shall eat straw like
    the ox.
8 The sucking child shall play over
    the hole of the asp,
  and the weaned child shall put his
    hand on the adder's den.
9 They shall not hurt or destroy
  in all my holy mountain;
  for the earth shall be full of the
    knowledge of the LORD
  as the waters cover the sea.

Reflecting on the Word

David's dynasty again seemed to be in jeopardy. Around 734 B.C. the armies of the northern kingdom (the region called Israel and Samaria in the New Testament) joined forces with the neighboring kingdom of Aram and Damascus (Syria). Together they tried to force Ahaz, the king of the southern kingdom of Judah, to become part of their alliance against Assyria. But Ahaz was afraid of being deposed by these armies and losing his throne. When Ahaz refused to join the coalition, Israel and Aram invaded Judah, with the intention of replacing Ahaz with a surrogate they could control. "[Ahaz's] heart and the heart of his people shook as the trees of the forest shake before the wind" at the invasion (Isaiah 7:2). In the face of Judah's distress, God reconfirmed the promises he had made to David and his descendants that his kingdom would endure forever.

With eyes that penetrated through the dark clouds of impending disaster to see the glory of God, the prophet Isaiah spoke God's word to King Ahaz. Isaiah assured him of God's protection and of the downfall of Damascus and Samaria (Isaiah 7:3-9). He told Ahaz to ask God for a sign to reassure him, but the king refused, saying that he did not want to tempt the Lord (7:10-12). With a sign from God, Ahaz would have been more obliged to trust him, something he was unwilling to do. Nonetheless, Isaiah again declared God's willingness to provide

a sign that would confirm God's continued faithfulness to David's line:

> The Lord himself will give you a sign. Behold, a young woman shall conceive and bear a son, and shall call his name Immanuel. He shall eat curds and honey when he knows how to refuse the evil and choose the good. For before the child knows how to refuse the evil and choose the good, the land before whose two kings you are in dread will be deserted. (7:14-16)

Ahaz chose to rely on his own judgment and sought an alliance with Assyria to protect his kingdom, but his decision eventually led to Judah's ruin anyway.

Perhaps God particularly chose the birth of a child as the sign he offered Ahaz because every newborn is a universal and enduring sign of hope for the human race. Christian tradition interprets the verses in Isaiah as a reference to Christ, but their immediate reference was likely to Hezekiah, the child that would be born to Ahaz's wife, the queen mother. Hezekiah's birth ensured that another of David's line would sit on the throne, and before he was fully grown Damascus and Samaria had indeed fallen.

But the prophecy's fullest meaning came to pass when the Christ Child was born to the Virgin Mary (Matthew 1:18-25). God's Son—whose "name shall be called

Emmanuel, (which means, God with us)" (1:23)—would come in the flesh to dwell among us and bring us salvation and deliverance from sin and death. Jesus does not merely fulfill the prophetic expectations of God's people; he wildly exceeds them through his life and eternal reign.

The historical events described prophetically in Isaiah 9:7-20 follow the situation of Isaiah 7. The northern kingdom of Israel was invaded and conquered by the Assyrians. It was a time of great darkness for God's people as their land was devastated and they themselves were slain, deported, or reduced to poverty by their foreign enemies. This was, in part, a punishment for Israel's sins—of which Hosea and Amos and other contemporary prophets had warned.

But Isaiah's prophecy (9:2-7) shines brilliantly in the midst of Israel's desperate plight. These words, especially familiar to us from the first reading at the Christmas midnight liturgy, ring out with great hope and comfort: "The people who walked in darkness have seen a great light. . . . [T]he yoke of his burden . . . thou hast broken" (9:2, 4). God has not abandoned his people! With the coming of Christ, he has shattered the darkness and lifted from us the yoke of our sins.

The prophecy of Isaiah 9:6—"For to us a child is born, to us a son is given"—refers to the same child foretold in Isaiah 7. A partial fulfillment of Isaiah's words may be seen in the reign of King Hezekiah, Ahaz's succes-sor, who later led a religious reform of the southern kingdom (2 Chronicles 30:1-20). The titles given to the child are rich and full of prophetic significance. "Wonderful Counselor" points to one who with wisdom will carry out God's plans. "Mighty God" evokes the kingly image of one with the power to bring salvation. "Everlasting Father" calls to mind one who will be faithful to his people and care for them. "Prince of Peace" describes one whose reign ushers in harmony and complete accord. Thus, this oracle of hope unfolds a vision of a glorious king who will come to establish universal peace—one that Christians would later recognize as the God-man, Jesus Christ.

With the devastation of the northern kingdom—and later, the southern kingdom—David's dynasty did indeed seem to have been reduced to a dry stump, the hacked-off trunk of a once flourishing tree. However, in yet another prophecy Isaiah foretold that a descendant of David—a "shoot from the stump of Jesse [the father of David]" (Isaiah 11:1)—was still to spring forth. New life, vigorous and fruitful, would yet come forth from these withered roots.

Isaiah further described this ideal ruler as one anointed with the Spirit of God. Equipped to rule with the gifts of the Spirit, he would judge righteously and not be swayed by human concerns (Isaiah 11:2-5). Wisdom, understanding, counsel, might, knowledge, and fear of the Lord—these gifts of the Spirit are qualities belonging to God that he would bestow on his chosen one. Filled with the Spirit, God's anointed one would proclaim truth, administer justice, and defend the poor and afflicted.

Moreover, this ideal king would usher in an idyllic kingdom in which peace would reign. The image of the wolf and lamb, calf and lion existing together expresses the harmony of the messianic age (Isaiah 11:6-8). In this new era, "the earth shall be full of the knowledge of the LORD as the waters cover the sea" (11:9).

Isaiah 11:10-16 describes the work of the descendant of King David in terms of restor-ing the Davidic kingdom. Exiles will return home (11:11-12, 16), the divided kingdom will be reunited (11:13), and neighboring nations will be conquered (11:14). It will be a new exodus, a new beginning (11:15-16).

But it would only be in Jesus that the kingdom of God would be truly restored, as God had promised through Isaiah. The new and vigorous life of the root of Jesse would be made manifest in Christ. Jesus, the son of David (Matthew 21:9), filled with the Holy Spirit (Luke 4:1), would inaugurate a new reign of God on earth, a new covenant between God and his people.

Pondering the Word

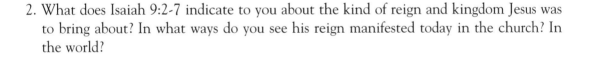

1. What images and metaphors are used in Isaiah 9:2-5 to describe the oppression and difficulties God's people were facing? What images did Isaiah use in these verses to describe salvation and deliverance? What emotions do you think these images stirred up in the Hebrew people?

_____

_____

_____

_____

_____

_____

_____

_____

_____

2. What does Isaiah 9:2-7 indicate to you about the kind of reign and kingdom Jesus was to bring about? In what ways do you see his reign manifested today in the church? In the world?

_____

_____

_____

_____

_____

_____

_____

_____

_____

3. Why does Isaiah use the term "zeal" in 9:7 in assuring us that God will bring about what he promises? How might this description shape your view of God and his nature?

_____

_____

_____

_____

_____

_____

_____

_____

_____

_____

_____

4. Why do you think Isaiah chose the seven particular gifts of the Spirit listed in 11:2-3? In what ways would these gifts empower a king? How did they empower Jesus?

_____

_____

_____

_____

_____

_____

_____

_____

_____

_____

_____

5. Note the attributes of the ideal ruler described in Isaiah 11:1-5. How will he carry out his rule? What will characterize his reign? How does this point to Jesus?

_____

_____

_____

_____

_____

_____

_____

_____

_____

_____

6. Isaiah 11:6-9 presents a beautiful picture of what an ideal world would be like. Which traditional enemies are reconciled? What does this suggest about God's desires for his kingdom?

_____

_____

_____

_____

_____

_____

_____

_____

_____

_____

Living the Word

1. When confronted with difficulties, how often are you inclined to rely on human resources —as King Ahaz did—to "save" yourself rather than rely on God and his promises? What could you do to deepen your trust in God?

_____

_____

_____

_____

_____

_____

_____

_____

_____

_____

2. Recall a situation when you felt that God gave you a sign assuring you of his love and care for you. What effect did this have on your relationship with God?

_____

_____

_____

_____

_____

_____

_____

_____

_____

_____

3. How has God's salvation shone forth like light in a dark area of your life? How have you experienced God freeing you from a "heavy yoke"?

_____

_____

_____

_____

_____

_____

_____

_____

_____

_____

4. Think of occasions when you experienced the Lord as Emmanuel, Wonderful Counselor, Mighty God, Everlasting Father, Prince of Peace. Which of these titles speaks to you most strongly right now? Why?

_____

_____

_____

_____

_____

_____

_____

_____

_____

_____

5. Reflect on the seven traditional gifts of the Holy Spirit listed in Isaiah 11:2-3, which were given to you in the Sacrament of Confirmation. What fruits of these gifts do you recognize in your life? How could you be more open to using the gifts that the Spirit has given you for others?

_____

_____

_____

_____

_____

_____

_____

_____

_____

_____

6. How does your image of heaven resemble the picture of Isaiah 11:6-9? What longings and desires of yours do you expect will be satisfied in heaven?

_____

_____

_____

_____

_____

_____

_____

_____

_____

Rooted in the Word

Jesus: A Portrait of the Spirit's Anointing

The ideal ruler foretold by Isaiah was to be anointed not only with oil but with the Spirit of God as well (Isaiah 11:2-5). Filled with the Spirit, this future king would defeat Israel's enemies and usher in a glorious reign of peace. Isaiah's prophecy was fulfilled in Jesus—called the "Christ," God's anointed one—when he was anointed by the Holy Spirit at his baptism. Each of the Evangelists, in describing this event (Matthew 3:16-17; Mark 1:9-11; Luke 3:21-22; John 1:32-34), notes the presence and role of the Spirit. This anointing marks the beginning of Jesus' messianic mission. Empowered by the Spirit, Jesus proclaimed the kingdom of God and carried out the Father's plan of redemption.

The name "Christian" is derived from this anointing. We followers of Christ are called Christians (*christianoi*), because we too are anointed (*chriometha*) with chrism, the "oil" of God, at baptism. As St. Athanasius, one of the early Fathers of the Church, wrote,

> The descent of the Holy Spirit on Jesus in the Jordan was for our benefit . . . to make us holy, so that we might share in his anointing and of us it might be said: "Do you not know that you are the temple of God and that the Spirit of God dwells in you" (1 Corinthians 3:16). For when the Lord, as a human being, was washed in the Jordan, we were the ones to be washed, in him and by him, and when he received the Spirit, we were the ones who, thanks to the Lord, were made recipients of the Spirit. (*Oratio 1 contra Arianos*)

Read and prayerfully reflect on these additional Scripture passages that describe the Spirit at work in and through Jesus and how the Spirit has been given to us also:

> [The Lord said to his people:]
> "I will pour out my spirit on all
>   flesh;
> your sons and your daughters shall
>   prophesy,
>   your old men shall dream dreams,
>   and your young men shall see
>   visions.
> Even upon the menservants and
>   maidservants
>   in those days, I will pour out my
>   spirit.
> (Joel 2:28-29)

John [the Baptist] bore witness, "I saw the Spirit descend as a dove from heaven, and it remained on him. I myself did not know him; but he who sent me to baptize with water said to

me, 'He on whom you see the Spirit descend and remain, this is he who baptizes with the Holy Spirit.' And I have seen and have borne witness that this is the Son of God."
(John 1:32-34)

[Jesus] breathed on [the disciples], and said to them, "Receive the Holy Spirit." (John 20:22)

When the day of Pentecost had come, they were all together in one place. And suddenly a sound came from heaven like the rush of a mighty wind, and it filled all the house where they were sitting.

And there appeared to them tongues as of fire, distributed and resting on each one of them. And they were all filled with the Holy Spirit and began to speak in other tongues, as the Spirit gave them utterance. (Acts 2:1-4)

Peter said to [those gathered on Pentecost], "Repent, and be baptized every one of you in the name of Jesus Christ for the forgiveness of your sins; and you shall receive the gift of the Holy Spirit. For the promise is to you and to your children and to all that are far off, every one whom the Lord our God calls to him." (Acts 2:38-39)

Treasuring the Word

A Reading from *Theotókos: Woman, Mother, Disciple* by Pope John Paul II

Isaiah's Prophecy Is Fulfilled in the Incarnation

"Behold, a virgin shall conceive and bear a son, and shall call his name Emmanuel" (Isaiah 7:14).

During the annunciation of the angel, who invited Joseph to take to himself Mary, his wife, "for that which is conceived in her is of the Holy Spirit," Matthew gives a Christological and Marian significance to the prophecy. He adds: "All this took place to fulfill what the Lord had spoken by the prophet: 'Behold, a virgin shall conceive and bear a son, and his name shall be called Emmanuel' (which means God-with-us)" (Matthew 1:22-23).

In the Hebrew text this prophecy does not explicitly foretell the virginal birth of Emmanuel: the word used (*almah*) simply means "a young woman," not necessarily a virgin. Moreover, we know that Jewish tradition did not hold up the idea of perpetual virginity, nor did it ever express the idea of virginal motherhood.

In the Greek tradition, however, the Hebrew word was translated *parthenos*—virgin. In this fact, which could seem merely a peculiarity of translation, we must recognize a mysterious orientation given by the Holy Spirit to Isaiah's words in order to prepare for the understanding of the Messiah's extraordinary birth. The translation of the word as "virgin" is explained by the fact that Isaiah's text solemnly prepares for the announcement of the conception and presents it as a divine sign (Isaiah 7:10-14), arousing the expectation of an extraordinary conception. It is not something extraordinary for a young woman to conceive a son after being joined to the husband. Such a formulation, then, suggests the interpretation given later in the Greek version. . . .

In the annunciation of the wondrous birth of Emmanuel, the indication of the woman who conceives and gives birth shows a certain intention to associate the mother with the destiny of the son—a prince destined to establish an ideal kingdom, the "messianic" kingdom—and offers a glimpse of a special divine plan, which highlights the woman's role. The sign is not only the child, but the extraordinary conception revealed later in the birth itself, a hope-filled event, which stresses the central role of the mother.

The prophecy of Emmanuel must also be understood in the horizon opened by the promise made to David, a promise we read about in the Second Book of Samuel. Here the prophet Nathan promises the king God's favor toward David's descendant; "He shall build a house for my name, and I will establish the throne of his kingdom forever. I will be his father, and he shall be my son" (2 Samuel 7:13-14). God wants to exercise a paternal role toward David's offspring, a role that will reveal its full, authentic meaning in the New Testament with the Incarnation of the Son of God in the family of David (cf. Romans 1:3).

In another very familiar text, the same prophet Isaiah confirms the unusual nature of Emmanuel's birth. Here are his words: "For to us a child is born, to us a son is given, and the government will be upon his shoulder, and he will be called 'Wonderful Counselor, Mighty God, Everlasting Father, Prince of Peace'" (9:6). Thus, in the series of names given the child, the prophet expresses the qualities of his royal office: wisdom, might, fatherly kindness, peacemaking. The mother is no longer mentioned here, but the exaltation of the son, who brings the people all they can hope for in the messianic kingdom, is also reflected in the woman who conceived him and gave him birth. . . .

The Old Testament does not contain a formal announcement of the virginal motherhood, which was fully revealed only by the New Testament. Nevertheless, Isaiah's prophecy (Isaiah 7:14) prepared for the revelation of this mystery and was construed so in the Greek translation of the Old Testament. By quoting the prophecy thus translated, Matthew's Gospel proclaims its perfect fulfillment through the conception of Jesus in Mary's virginal womb.

"You Shall Call His Name Jesus"

To you is born this day in the city of David a Savior, who is Christ the Lord.
Luke 2:11

It is awesome . . . that a poor little human creature, our sister human being, had the tremendous honor of forming a body and bringing God into the world. She received him, she guarded him, she enclosed him in the humble, narrow limits of her own body. What a privilege!
Père Jacques (Lucien-Louis Bunel),
Père Jacques: Resplendent in Victory

The Word Made Flesh

Mary, pregnant virgin!
Of what did you think
as you carried God beneath your heart,
bone of your bone,
flesh of your flesh?

Did you dream of
Israel restored
and David's son upon a royal throne?

II
Mary, virgin mother!
Of what did you think
as you gently laid your babe
against the manger's wood?

Did you already see his infant hands
(bone of your bone,
flesh of your flesh)
stretched to the beam of a cross,
nailed to the wood of a tree?
In your son's birth cry
(God's word given voice in the wails of a newborn),
did you already hear the last cry
that would be wrenched from him at death:
"It is finished"?

III
Mary, full of grace!
Of what do you now think
as you gaze upon your son in glory,
his wounds still pleading on our behalf before the throne of God?

For Jesus,
bone of your bone,
flesh of your flesh,
has triumphed over sin and death
and crushed the serpent's head.

Blessed are you, Mary, among all women,
and blessed is the fruit of your womb!

Matthew 1:18-25 The Scene

¹⁸Now the birth of Jesus Christ took place in this way. When his mother Mary had been betrothed to Joseph, before they came together she was found to be with child of the Holy Spirit; ¹⁹and her husband Joseph, being a just man and unwilling to put her to shame, resolved to send her away quietly. ²⁰But as he considered this, behold, an angel of the Lord appeared to him in a dream, saying, "Joseph, son of David, do not fear to take Mary your wife, for that which is conceived in her is of the Holy Spirit; ²¹she will bear a son, and you shall call his name Jesus, for he will save his people from their sins."

²²All this took place to fulfil what the Lord had spoken by the prophet:

²³ "Behold, a virgin shall conceive and
       bear a son,
   and his name shall be called
       Emmanuel"

(which means, God with us). ²⁴When Joseph woke from sleep, he did as the angel of the Lord commanded him; he took his wife, ²⁵but knew her not until she had borne a son; and he called his name Jesus.

Luke 2:1-21 The Scene

¹In those days a decree went out from Caesar Augustus that all the world should be enrolled. ²This was the first enrollment, when Quirinius was governor of Syria. ³And all went to be enrolled, each to his own city. ⁴And Joseph also went up from Galilee, from the city of Nazareth, to Judea, to the city of David, which is called Bethlehem, because he was of the house and lineage of David, ⁵to be enrolled with Mary, his betrothed, who was with child. ⁶And while they were there, the time came for her to be delivered.

⁷And she gave birth to her first-born son and wrapped him in swaddling cloths, and laid him in a manger, because there was no place for them in the inn.

⁸And in that region there were shepherds out in the field, keeping watch over their flock by night. ⁹And an angel of the Lord appeared to them, and the glory of the Lord shone around them, and they were filled with fear. ¹⁰And the angel said to them, "Be not afraid; for behold, I bring you good news of a

great joy which will come to all the people; [11]for to you is born this day in the city of David a Savior, who is Christ the Lord. [12]And this will be a sign for you: you will find a babe wrapped in swaddling cloths and lying in a manger." [13]And suddenly there was with the angel a multitude of the heavenly host praising God and saying,

[14] "Glory to God in the highest,
    and on earth peace among men with
        whom he is pleased!"

[15]When the angels went away from them into heaven, the shepherds said to one another, "Let us go over to Bethlehem and see this thing that has happened, which the Lord has made known to us." [16]And they went with haste, and found Mary and Joseph, and the babe lying in a manger. [17]And when they saw it they made known the saying which had been told them concerning this child; [18]and all who heard it wondered at what the shepherds told them. [19]But Mary kept all these things, pondering them in her heart. [20]And the shepherds returned, glorifying and praising God for all they had heard and seen, as it had been told them.

[21]And at the end of eight days, when he was circumcised, he was called Jesus, the name given by the angel before he was conceived in the womb.

Reflecting on the Word

The moment long awaited by Israel is now at hand. Devout Jews had been yearning for centuries for the fulfillment of the messianic promises. Their hopes and expectations—and much more—would soon be realized: "When the time had fully come, God sent forth his Son, born of woman, born under the law, to redeem those who were under the law, so that we might receive adoption as sons" (Galatians 4:4-5). Another English translation, "In the fullness of time," evokes the vivid image of year being added to year, like an empty measure being filled drop by drop until it brims over.

"Born of woman"—God chose to send one of human flesh and blood to overcome the curse of sin that Adam and Eve had brought upon humankind. And so he asked a daughter of Israel, Mary of Nazareth, to be the mother of his Son. Of Mary's role in God's plan, Cardinal John Henry Newman noted,

> The Seed of the woman, announced to guilty Eve, after long delay, was at length appearing upon earth, and was to be born of her. In her the destinies of the world were to be reversed, and the serpent's head bruised. On her was bestowed the greatest honor ever put upon any individual of our fallen race. God was taking upon Him her flesh, and humbling Himself to be called her offspring;—such is the deep mystery! (Sermon 12, "The Reverence Due to the Virgin")

Mary gave her consent to God's request—"Behold, I am the handmaid of the Lord; let it be to me according to your word" (Luke 1:38)—and Jesus was conceived in her womb through the overshadowing of the Holy Spirit (1:35). Yet Mary must have been overwhelmed as she heard the angel Gabriel describe the child she was to bear: he was to be named Jesus (1:31), meaning "the Lord saves," and would be called "Son of the Most High" (1:32) and "Son of God" (1:35). He would be the fulfillment of the promise God made to David so long ago (1:32-33).

Matthew tells us that Joseph took Mary, his betrothed, to be his wife after God assured him of the divine purpose at work in her. The child Mary was carrying had been conceived in a way that surpassed nature—"of the Holy Spirit" (Matthew 1:18)—and would "save his people from their sins" (1:21). "[Joseph] took Mary as his wife in humble acceptance of the mystery of her maternity. He accepted her along with her Son who would come to the world by the action of the Holy Spirit. St. Joseph can therefore be compared to Our Lady in his great docility to the will of God as revealed to him by an angel" (Pope John Paul II, *Guardian of the Redeemer*).

Matthew's account of Jesus' birth begins with his genealogy (Matthew 1:1-16). Jewish genealogies followed the male line. Joseph belonged to the family of David and was, as the husband of Mary, the legal father of Jesus. As such, God entrusted Joseph with the responsibility of naming the child (1:21, 25). Since this was a parental duty, Joseph's action indicates that he adopted this child into his lineage. Through Joseph's lineage and his legal paternity, Jesus is the son of David—and thus fulfills God's promise to David that his dynasty would last for all generations. Since it was common for people to marry within their clans, most likely Mary was also descended from the house of David.

But it is through the Holy Spirit and the miraculous virginal maternity of Mary that Jesus is the Son of God. Concerning the manner of Jesus' birth, Matthew refers back to the prophecy of Isaiah 7 and explains, "All this took place to fulfil what the Lord had spoken by the prophet: "Behold, a virgin shall conceive and bear a son, and his name shall be called Emmanuel" (which means, God with us)" (Matthew 1:22-23). Archbishop Oscar Romero pointed out that as the virgin mother of the Messiah, "Mary is the human instrument . . . who by her holiness was able to incarnate in history God's divine life" (*The Violence of Love*).

In words that have become so familiar to us that we know them by heart, Luke describes the journey of Joseph and Mary from Nazareth to Bethlehem, David's city, and the unassuming circumstances of Jesus' birth there (2:4-7).

Bethlehem lies in the Judean hills, six miles south of Jerusalem. Rachel, the wife of the patriarch Jacob, was buried there, and Ruth, who became the great-grandmother of David and ancestress of Jesus, settled in the town. Bethlehem was the birthplace of David as well as the place where Samuel anointed David king to succeed Saul. Bethlehem is a small and seemingly insignificant town, yet the prophet Micah, a contemporary of Isaiah in the latter half of the eighth century B.C., said of it,

> But you, O Bethlehem Ephrathah,
>   who are little to be among the
>   clans of Judah,
> from you shall come forth for me
>   one who is to be ruler in Israel,
> whose origin is from of old,
>   from ancient days.
> (5:2)

Jewish tradition interpreted Micah's prophecy as predicting the exact place of birth of the anticipated Messiah, a King who was to be far greater than David. Centuries after Micah, the Roman census decreed by Caesar Augustus brought Mary and Joseph to Bethlehem, where the birth of Jesus took place. Learned scribes of Israel who studied the ancient writings of the prophets recalled Micah's prediction of where the Christ was to be born when the wise men came to King Herod's palace seeking the newborn King of the Jews (Matthew 2:1-6). God's plan to redeem the human race, begun at the gates of Eden, reached now to the gates of Bethlehem.

The angel's message to the shepherds contains the announcement of the birth in the city of David of a "Savior, who is Christ the Lord" (Luke 2:11). This child is a savior, because he has come to redeem and save us from our sins. He is Christ (*christos* means anointed one), the Messiah now born in fulfillment of the ancient hopes. Yet the angel also told the shepherds that they would find this newborn "wrapped in swaddling cloths and lying in a manger" (2:12), a humble setting for one they announced so exaltedly. Luke's text echoes the description of Solomon, King David's son, found in the Book of Wisdom:

> And when I was born, I began to
>   breathe the common air,
> and fell upon the kindred earth,
> and my first sound was a cry, like
>   that of all.
> I was nursed with care in swaddling
>   cloths.

> For no king has had a different
>   beginning of existence;
> there is for all mankind one
>   entrance into life, and a
>   common departure.
> (7:3-6)

By his human birth Jesus, Son of God and son of Mary, shared our common humanity, our vulnerability, our mortality.

The humility of God condescending to being born as a human child in a stable is almost unfathomable. Jesus' birth in the flesh is a manifestation of the mercy and grace of God. The shepherds were privileged to be the first to greet the incarnate God and to testify of him to others (Luke 2:17-18). Surely what they saw that wondrous night transformed their lives and set them aglow with hope, for now a child was growing up among them to be their savior!

Mary "kept all these things, pondering them in her heart" (Luke 2:19) through the years ahead as her son grew and God's unlikely plan of salvation unfolded before her.

Pondering the Word

1. Summarize Joseph's role in God's plan of salvation. What does the narrative in Matthew 1:18-25 indicate to you about Joseph's character? What qualities does he exhibit?

_____

_____

_____

_____

_____

_____

_____

_____

_____

2. List all the titles attributed to Jesus in Matthew 1:18-25 and Luke 2:1-21. Why, in your opinion, did Matthew and Luke begin their gospels with such attention to Jesus' identity?

_____

_____

_____

_____

_____

_____

_____

_____

_____

3. Identify the links between David and Jesus recorded by Matthew and Luke. Why do you think the Evangelists pointed so frequently to the Old Testament prophecies in describing Jesus and his birth?

_____

_____

_____

_____

_____

_____

_____

_____

_____

_____

4. Luke mentions many concrete details about the circumstances surrounding Jesus' birth (the Roman census, the city of David, the lack of space in the inn). Do you think Mary and Joseph understood the significance of these circumstances at the time? What does this physical setting add to your understanding of Jesus' birth and mission?

_____

_____

_____

_____

_____

_____

_____

_____

_____

_____

5. Why, in your opinion, did God announce the birth of his Son to shepherds rather than to the leaders of Israel? Note the verbs that describe the shepherds' actions. What do these actions and their response to God's message suggest about them?

_____

_____

_____

_____

_____

_____

_____

_____

_____

_____

6. What is the significance of Jesus' incarnation—that is, of the fact that he took on human flesh to redeem us? How is this related to God's promise in Genesis 3:15?

_____

_____

_____

_____

_____

_____

_____

_____

_____

_____

Living the Word

1. How does the fact that Jesus is both God and man affect you personally? Have you ever felt reluctant to bring your troubles to Jesus, thinking that he wouldn't understand? If so, how can you overcome that reluctance?

_____

_____

_____

_____

_____

_____

_____

_____

_____

_____

2. Israel awaited the coming of the Messiah for long centuries, until "the time had fully come" (Galatians 4:4) for God to send his Son. Reflect on a situation in your life in which you had to wait on God and his timing. How did you deal with it? How can "waiting on God" be an active rather than a passive activity?

_____

_____

_____

_____

_____

_____

_____

_____

_____

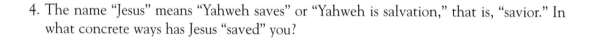

3. Joseph trusted God and obeyed him in the face of unexpected situations such as Mary's miraculous pregnancy and the lack of accommodations in Bethlehem. What current situations in your life call for trust in God and obedience? How can Joseph's example help you?

_____

_____

_____

_____

_____

_____

_____

_____

_____

_____

4. The name "Jesus" means "Yahweh saves" or "Yahweh is salvation," that is, "savior." In what concrete ways has Jesus "saved" you?

_____

_____

_____

_____

_____

_____

_____

_____

_____

_____

5. The shepherds shared the good news of what they had been told by the angel with Mary and Joseph and others (Luke 2:17-18). Have you ever had the opportunity to share Christ and the gospel message with others? Can you think of instances when you missed an opportunity to spread the good news? What prevented you?

_____

_____

_____

_____

_____

_____

_____

_____

_____

6. At the birth of Christ, a heavenly host of angels sang, "Glory to God in the highest" (Luke 2:13-14). Imagine yourself joining in their song of worship, and write your own prayer praising God for his Son's incarnation and thanking him for his great love for you.

_____

_____

_____

_____

_____

_____

_____

_____

_____

Jesus: A Portrait of Humility

Who is more helpless than a new-born child? Yet Jesus did not hesitate to share in our humanity, and his birth was only the first manifestation of his humility—that self-emptying which he freely embraced for our sake, for the forgiveness of our sins. For "Christ Jesus, . . . though he was in the form of God, did not count equality with God a thing to be grasped, but emptied himself, taking the form of a servant, being born in the likeness of men" (Philippians 2:5-7). As Theodotus of Ancyra explained so eloquently in a homily he preached at the Council of Ephesus (A.D. 431),

> The Lord of all comes in the form of a servant. He comes as a poor man, so that he will not frighten away those people he is trying to capture like a huntsman. He is born in an obscure town, deliberately choosing a humble dwelling place. His mother is an ordinary girl, not some great lady. And the reason for all this lowly state is so that he may gently ensnare mankind and bring us to salvation. If he had been born amid the splendor of a rich family, unbelievers would surely have said that the face of the world had been changed by the power of wealth. If he had chosen to be born in Rome, the greatest of cities, they would have ascribed the change to the power of her citizens. . . . [But] he chose nothing but poverty and mean surroundings, everything that was plain and ordinary and (in the eyes of most people) obscure. And this was so that it could be clearly seen that it was the Godhead alone that was to transform the world. ("On the Day of the Lord's Nativity")

Jesus' humility was not only manifested in his birth, but through his entire life—and, most significantly, in his death. He lived the life of a common man and set the example for us to follow in our service to one another. Finally, "he humbled himself and became obedient unto death, even death on a cross" (Philippians 2:8).

Read and prayerfully reflect on these additional Scripture passages describing Christ's example of humble servanthood and the humility that we, too, are called to imitate:

> Thus says the LORD:
> "This is the man to whom I will look,
>   he that is humble and contrite in
>   spirit,
>   and trembles at my word."
> (Isaiah 66:2)

[Jesus said:] "Whoever humbles himself like this child, he is the greatest in the kingdom of heaven." (Matthew 18:4)

[Jesus said:] "He who is greatest among you shall be your servant; whoever exalts himself will be humbled, and whoever humbles himself will be exalted." (Matthew 23:11-12)

Jesus called [the apostles] to him and said to them, "You know that those who are supposed to rule over the Gentiles lord it over them, and their great men exercise authority over them. But it shall not be so among you; but whoever would be great among you must be your servant, and whoever would be first among you must be slave of all. For the Son of man also came not to be served but to serve, and to give his life as a ransom for many." (Mark 10:42-45)

Clothe yourselves, all of you, with humility toward one another, for "God opposes the proud, but gives grace to the humble." Humble yourselves therefore under the mighty hand of God, that in due time he may exalt you. (1 Peter 5:5-6)

Treasuring the Word

A Reading from *The Coming of God* by Maria Boulding, OSB

The Risk of Promise

Rejoice," says the angel to Mary at the Annunciation, echoing the note of messianic joy struck by the prophet Zephaniah, who had spoken to the "people humble and lowly" whom the Lord would cherish in Israel:

> Sing aloud, O daughter Zion: shout,
> O Israel!
> Rejoice and exult with all your heart,
> O daughter Jerusalem! . . .
> The king of Israel, the LORD, is in
> your midst.
> (Zephaniah 3:14-15)

Mary is presented as the Daughter of Zion, as Israel at the moment of its highest responsiveness to God, as the place where salvation will be revealed. The lifelines of hope converge in her and in the promise she receives. Her child is to inherit the throne of his father David, and will reign for ever; the angel's words recall the prophecy of Nathan to David concerning the permanence of his dynasty. The power of the Most High will "overshadow" Mary, as in the Old Testament the cloud was the sign of Yahweh's presence and his glory filled the tabernacle from within. As a confirming sign, Mary is told of the unlooked-for conception of a son by her cousin Elizabeth, for "nothing will be impossible with God" (Luke 1:37); the words echo Genesis 18:14 where an angelic visitor, having promised a son to the elderly couple, Abraham and Sarah, meets Sarah's skepticism with the question, "Is anything too wonderful for the LORD?" Mary is like the new Ark of the Covenant, the place of God's dwelling with his people, and when she visits Elizabeth the unborn John "leaps," as David had leaped and danced before the Ark. Mary's child is to be called Jesus, a name which corresponds to Joshua, "Yahweh saves."

All this is beautiful, and we may well stand back and marvel. Nothing has been wasted or lost; all the agonies and disappointments have been worth while. The overarching wisdom of God has carried the plan through, and now the Messiah for whom Israel longed is to be welcomed by this poor, silent, humble girl who represents her people. Such a reading is wholly legitimate, indeed necessary; it is what the evangelist intends, but it is important to remember that we read, as Luke wrote, with benefit of hindsight. In the full light of Easter and Pentecost and the Church's pondering of the mystery of Christ, Luke could write the Annunciation story in this poetic, allusive, theologically developed way, and we rejoice in it, but to the people within the story it did not look like that.

As the poor and faithful of Israel had said "Yes" to God in anguish of spirit, not seeing how things could work out but conscious only of the tearing away from what had gone before and the venture forward into the dark unknown at God's word, so Mary was being asked to make the leap of faith in response to God's self-offer and invitation. There were no models for understanding, no conforming precedents, because this thing had never happened before. The flesh-taking of the Son of God was much more than a fulfillment of Israel's expectations, much more than a satisfactory tying-up of all the strands of hope; it was the un-heard-of gift, the breaking in of the wholly new thing.

Like the prophets and the anonymous believers before her, she let go of familiar, intelligible patterns and ways of relating to God and the universe, of those frameworks which had genuinely supported meaning hitherto, and were indeed God-given. She said her "Yes" to the Beyond, she let go of her securities, faced the misunderstanding, bore the shame, accepted her own bewilderment and risk. She was herself reborn to a new existence, that she might bring forth life for many. There was joy for her, and in the newness of life she danced with the Beyond that was within.

Herald of the Messiah

In those days came John the Baptist, preaching in the wilderness of Judea, "Repent, for the kingdom of heaven is at hand."
Matthew 3:1-2

The voice of John still resounds in the Gospels as coming from a desert region in which the transcendent God dwells in all his holiness. He embodies in his life as well as in his speech as it were, the majesty and purity of the living God.
John Eudes Bamberger, OCSO,
Homily, 14 December 2000

Prepare the Way of the Lord

Prepare the way of the Lord,
make his paths straight.
Prepare my heart, O Lord,
and pave the way for your coming.
Invade and flood me with your Spirit,
and fill the spaces you carve out in me with your own presence.

Every valley shall be filled.
Fill in those depressions dug so deeply in the heart
by distrust
or desperation
or dreams that only disappoint.

Every mountain and hill shall be brought low.
Cast down those peaks that loom over me
of pride
and pettiness
and promises broken or unkept by me.

The crooked shall be made straight.
Make whole and straight what is out of shape:
the truth that's bent by my little lies,
the troubled thoughts that wind their way so tortuously through my mind,
and the timidity that deforms my heart (and cheats others of my love).

The rough ways shall be made smooth;
and all flesh shall see the salvation of God.
Remove the stones that block my way
and make level a path for my feet
that I not stumble as I run to you!

St. John the Baptist, pray for me!

Matthew 3:1-17 *The Scene*

[1]In those days came John the Baptist, preaching in the wilderness of Judea, [2]"Repent, for the kingdom of heaven is at hand." [3]For this is he who was spoken of by the prophet Isaiah when he said,

> "The voice of one crying in the
>   wilderness:
> Prepare the way of the Lord,
> make his paths straight."

[4]Now John wore a garment of camel's hair, and a leather girdle around his waist; and his food was locusts and wild honey. [5]Then went out to him Jerusalem and all Judea and all the region about the Jordan, [6]and they were baptized by him in the river Jordan, confessing their sins. [7]But when he saw many of the Pharisees and Sadducees coming for baptism, he said to them, "You brood of vipers! Who warned you to flee from the wrath to come? [8]Bear fruit that befits repentance, [9]and do not presume to say to yourselves, 'We have Abraham as our father'; for I tell you, God is able from these stones to raise up children to Abraham. [10]Even now the axe is laid to the root of the trees; every tree therefore that does not bear good fruit is cut down and thrown into the fire.

[11]"I baptize you with water for repentance, but he who is coming after me is mightier than I, whose sandals I am not worthy to carry; he will baptize you with the Holy Spirit and with fire. [12]His winnowing fork is in his hand, and he will clear his threshing floor and gather his wheat into the granary, but the chaff he will burn with unquenchable fire."

[13]Then Jesus came from Galilee to the Jordan to John, to be baptized by him. [14]John would have prevented him, saying, "I need to be baptized by you, and do you come to me?" [15]But Jesus answered him, "Let it be so now; for thus it is fitting for us to fulfill all righteousness." Then he consented. [16]And when Jesus was baptized, he went up immediately from the water, and behold, the heavens were opened and he saw the Spirit of God descending like a dove, and alighting on him; [17]and lo, a voice from heaven, saying, "This is my beloved Son, with whom I am well pleased."

**See also Mark 1:1-11;
Luke 3:1-17, 21-22;
John 1:6-8, 19-34**

Matthew 11:2-15 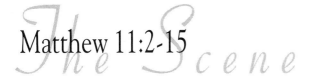 The Scene

²Now when John heard in prison about the deeds of the Christ, he sent word by his disciples ³and said to him, "Are you he who is to come, or shall we look for another?" ⁴And Jesus answered them, "Go and tell John what you hear and see: ⁵the blind receive their sight and the lame walk, lepers are cleansed and the deaf hear, and the dead are raised up, and the poor have good news preached to them. ⁶And blessed is he who takes no offense at me."

⁷As they went away, Jesus began to speak to the crowds concerning John: "What did you go out into the wilderness to behold? A reed shaken by the wind? ⁸Why then did you go out? To see a man clothed in soft raiment? Behold, those who wear soft raiment are in kings' houses. ⁹Why then did you go out? To see a prophet? Yes, I tell you, and more than a prophet. ¹⁰This is he of whom it is written,

'Behold, I send my messenger
    before thy face,
who shall prepare thy way before
    thee.'

¹¹Truly, I say to you, among those born of women there has risen no one greater than John the Baptist; yet he who is least in the kingdom of heaven is greater than he. ¹²From the days of John the Baptist until now the kingdom of heaven has suffered violence, and men of violence take it by force. ¹³For all the prophets and the law prophesied until John; ¹⁴and if you are willing to accept it, he is Elijah who is to come. ¹⁵He who has ears to hear, let him hear."

See also Luke 7:18-35

Reflecting on the Word

John the Baptist reached beyond himself, both backward and forward in time. He represented the history of Israel, waiting for the fulfillment of God's promise to send a messiah. And he pointed to the future, announcing the coming of the Messiah who would establish the reign of God. John stood at the threshold between the Old and New Testaments, a bridge linking the two. In him we see the culmination of centuries of prophecy, anticipation, and preparation. He is the last of the prophets announcing Jesus from afar, and the first of the witnesses to Jesus, actually pointing him out.

The Baptist appeared out of the desert in the spirit and power of Elijah (2 Kings 1:8; Matthew 11:14; Luke 1:17). Not only was John foreshadowed in Elijah, a prophet consumed with zeal for the glory of the Lord, but his coming and role were foretold by Isaiah and Malachi. John fulfilled Isaiah's prophecy of the voice of one crying in the wilderness (Isaiah 40:3) as he came proclaiming a call to repentance. And Malachi had announced a coming day of judgment, the "day of the Lord," which was to be preceded by a special emissary of God: "Behold, I send my messenger to prepare the way before me. . . . [H]e is like a refiner's fire and like fuller's soap" (3:1-2).

John broke the prophetic silence that had followed Malachi for several hundred years. Although his message was like that of the great Old Testament prophets who had so often called Israel to repentance, John went even further: He proclaimed that the kingdom of God was now at hand and exhorted his hearers to prepare for it by purifying their hearts.

Who was this man, the one whom Jesus himself called the greatest of those born of women, yet least among all those in the kingdom of God (Matthew 11:11)? John was the son of Zechariah and Elizabeth, who were "both righteous before God, walking in all the commandments and ordinances of the Lord blameless" (Luke 1:6). But the couple was childless; Elizabeth was sterile, and she and her husband were "advanced in years" (1:7).

In Jewish society childlessness was a particular sorrow because it ruled out the couple as potential parents or ancestors of the expected Messiah. Barrenness was considered a shame or even, at times, a punishment for sin. However, Zechariah and Elizabeth's disappointment did not estrange them from God. Zechariah continually made his plea to God for a child, and God answered in an extraordinary way (Luke 1:8-17).

Even while John was in his mother's womb, he began his lifelong mission of announcing the coming of the Lord. When Mary, pregnant with the child Jesus, visited Elizabeth, John leapt for joy in the womb in recognition of the presence of the redeemer (Luke 1:41). Zechariah's canticle of praise (1:67-79), uttered in the Holy Spirit at the wondrous birth of his son, vibrates with hope and expectation as Israel stands on the verge of seeing God's promise fulfilled: "You, child, will be called the prophet of the Most High; for you will go before the Lord to prepare his ways" (1:76).

The New Testament is succinct in describing the years between John's birth and the beginning of his public ministry: "The child grew and became strong in spirit, and he was in the wilderness till the day of his manifestation to Israel" (Luke 1:80). Yet we can suppose that John was raised in the traditions of contemporary Judaism. Gabriel's directives to Zechariah that the child never drink wine or strong drink (1:15) indicate that John was set apart for the Lord.

John lived in the wilderness, being formed in communion with God to fulfill his role as herald of the Messiah. In the desert—where he was disciplined in prayer, fasting, and detachment from the material world—his focus was on God alone: As St. Jerome put it, "John lived in the desert, and his eyes, searching for Christ, refused to see anything but him."

John dressed in camel's hair, girded with a leather belt, and survived on locusts and wild honey (Matthew 3:4; Mark 1:6). The austerity of the desert strengthened him for his mission. In the wilderness John's ear was attuned to the voice of God, alert to the Spirit who told him about the one who was to follow him. During those years in the desert, John's longing to see the Messiah he was to proclaim must have grown in maturity and vitality. He, the friend of the bridegroom (John 3:29), eagerly awaited the moment when he could cry out, "Behold, the bridegroom comes."

In ancient times, when a king traveled from place to place, messengers ran ahead to announce his coming and encourage the people to prepare to receive the royal visitor. Messengers did not take this role upon themselves, but were appointed to it. So too was John an envoy, a herald chosen by God to announce his reign and the imminent coming of his Son.

After centuries of waiting, imagine Israel's heightened sense of expectancy! People flocked to the desert to see John and hear what he was preaching. Because he attracted great crowds—Pharisees and Sadducees as well as common people—his influence was widespread. As the first-century Jewish historian Josephus noted, "John called the Baptist . . . was a good man and had urged the Jews to exert themselves to virtue, both as to justice toward one another and reverence towards God. . . . [All the people] massed about him, for they were very greatly moved by his words. . . . They seemed ready to do any thing he should advise."

John made it clear that preparation for the coming of the Messiah demanded conversion of heart. He exhorted his listeners, "Bear fruit that befits repentance" (Matthew 3:8). It was not enough to stop sinning—the evidence of repentance must be apparent in the way one lives.

True to his mission as a herald, John neither claimed more than God assigned to him nor attempted to promote himself. He was willing to fulfill his role as forerunner and to step aside at Jesus' appearance; in fact, John even pointed his own disciples toward Jesus (John 1:35-41). The Baptist's humility and genuine readiness to step off center stage are clear in his final witness to Jesus: "He who has the bride is the bridegroom; the friend of the bridegroom, who stands and hears him, rejoices greatly at the bridegroom's voice; therefore this joy of mine is now full. He must increase, but I must decrease" (3:29-30).

Little is known of John's relationship with Jesus. We have no idea whether the two grew up with knowledge of one another, though Luke describes them as distant cousins (Luke 1:36). According to John's own testimony, he did not recognize Jesus to be the one whose coming he was proclaiming until he saw the Spirit rest upon him at his baptism (John 1:31-34).

How often did John and Jesus meet after Jesus began his public ministry? The gospels tell us nothing, though they record that the imprisoned John sent his disciples to Jesus to inquire about his messianic identity. In answer, Jesus pointed to his deeds and then gave public testimony that John was "more than a prophet" and was "Elijah who is to come" (Matthew 11:2-14). Finally, when John was beheaded by Herod (Matthew 14:1-12; Mark 6:14-29), Jesus went into the hills alone to grieve and pray (Matthew 14:13).

Even in death John continued to be a forerunner of Jesus. He was a Christian martyr before Christ himself was crucified. As the Jesuit missionary and author Fr. André Retif eloquently wrote,

Should we not say that John loved Christ in life and preceded him in death? Others have followed in the footsteps of Christ, but John, in this respect also, preceded Christ, who, we almost dare to say, walked in John's footsteps. It is certainly very hard for a friend of Christ to die without the help of his example and with no knowledge of his triumphant resurrection and glorious ascension. John had even this bitter cup to drink. He drained it before his Master; and it almost seems, if it be possible, that he wanted to encourage him in death. (*John the Baptist: Missionary of Christ*)

John's message did not die with him. The church honors John with many titles that reflect how faithfully he carried out his mission: Witness of the Lord, Voice of the Word, Precursor of Truth, Crown of the Prophets, Forerunner of the Redeemer, Preparer of Salvation, Light of the Martyrs, and Servant of the Word. His call still reaches us today: "Bear fruit that befits repentance."

Pondering the Word

1. All four gospels apply the words of Isaiah 40:3 to John the Baptist—Matthew 3:3; Mark 1:3; Luke 3:4; John 1:23. In what specific ways did John "prepare the way" for the Messiah and thus fulfill Isaiah's prophecy? What are the main elements of John the Baptist's message?

_____

_____

_____

_____

_____

_____

_____

_____

_____

_____

2. Who were among those who came to hear John the Baptist preach (Matthew 3:5, 7; Luke 3:10, 12, 14)? How did he challenge them? Of what did he warn them? What did he say that repentance and conversion require? Note the phrases that indicate how John's listeners responded.

_____

_____

_____

_____

_____

_____

_____

_____

_____

3. Why did Jesus ask John to baptize him? How did John react to Jesus' request? What does this suggest to you about Jesus? About John? What is the significance of the events that occurred at Jesus' baptism?

_____

_____

_____

_____

_____

_____

_____

_____

_____

_____

4. Why, in your opinion, did John send his disciples to question Jesus (Matthew 11:2-3)? What do you think John understood about Jesus and his mission? What kind of Messiah do you think John expected Jesus to be?

_____

_____

_____

_____

_____

_____

_____

_____

_____

5. How did Jesus describe John the Baptist (Matthew 11:7-15; John 5:35)? Why do you think Jesus said that the "least in the kingdom of God" is greater than John?

_____

_____

_____

_____

_____

_____

_____

_____

_____

6. What symbol or image would you choose to illustrate John's life or character? Why?

_____

_____

_____

_____

_____

_____

_____

_____

_____

Living the Word

1. What aspect of John the Baptist's life or activities speaks most directly to you? Why? What personal lesson have you learned from his example?

_____
_____
_____
_____
_____
_____
_____
_____
_____

2. John was sensitive and open to the Holy Spirit. Think of an occasion when you were led or prompted by the Spirit to do something. Was it difficult for you to respond? If so, why? What happened?

_____
_____
_____
_____
_____
_____
_____
_____
_____

3. John's message was one of conversion: "Repent. . . . Bear fruit that befits repentance" (Matthew 3:2, 8). In what areas of your life do you recognize the fruits of repentance?

_____

_____

_____

_____

_____

_____

_____

_____

_____

4. St. Paul said, "It is no longer I who live, but Christ who lives in me" (Galatians 2:20). In what way is this statement similar to John's desire to "decrease" so that Jesus could "increase" (John 3:30)? What are some concrete ways you could "decrease" so that Christ might "increase" in you?

_____

_____

_____

_____

_____

_____

_____

_____

_____

5. John prepared the way for the coming of the Lord. How can you prepare your heart to receive the Lord in a deeper way?

_____

_____

_____

_____

_____

_____

_____

_____

_____

_____

6. John was a man who was truly free—free from fear of the opinion of others, and free to direct all his energies to announcing Jesus. Do you feel like a person who is truly free to do God's will? Is there anything holding you back?

_____

_____

_____

_____

_____

_____

_____

_____

_____

_____

Rooted in the Word

Jesus: A Portrait of the Word Sent by God

John's role was to "bear witness to the light, that all might believe through him. He was not the light, but came to bear witness to the light" (John 1:7-8). That light is "the true light that enlightens every man"—the Word who was made flesh in our midst (1:9, 14). As St. Augustine distinguished between John and the incarnate Christ, "John is the voice, but the Lord is the Word who was in the beginning. John is the voice that lasts for a time; from the beginning Christ is the Word who lives for ever."

Jesus, the Word-made-flesh, was sent by God to reconcile us to himself. "By giving us, as he did, his Son, his only Word, he has in that one Word said everything. . . . Although he had spoken but partially through the prophets he has now said everything in Christ. He has given us everything, his own Son" (St. John of the Cross, *The Ascent of Mount Carmel*).

Read and prayerfully reflect on these additional Scripture passages to enhance your understanding of how Jesus, the Word of the Father, was sent into the world as the Redeemer-Messiah to fulfill his plan of salvation:

> Jesus said to [his disciples], "My food is to do the will of him who sent me, and to accomplish his work." (John 4:34)

> Jesus said [to the Jews who had believed in him], "If God were your Father, you would love me, for I proceeded and came forth from God; I came not of my own accord, but he sent me. (John 8:42)

> [Peter addressed the people:] "[W]hat God foretold by the mouth of all the prophets, that his Christ should suffer, he thus fulfilled. Repent therefore, and turn again, that your sins may be blotted out, that times of refreshing may come from the presence of the Lord, and that he may send the Christ appointed for you, Jesus, whom heaven must receive until the time for establishing all that God spoke by the mouth of his holy prophets from of old. Moses said, 'The Lord God will raise up for you a prophet from your brethren as he raised me up. You shall listen to him in whatever he tells you.' . . . God, having raised up his servant, sent him to you first, to bless you in turning every one of you from your wickedness." (Acts 3:18-22, 26)

> In many and various ways God spoke of old to our fathers by the prophets; but in these last days he has spoken to us by a Son, whom he appointed the heir of all things, through whom also he created

the world. He reflects the glory of God and bears the very stamp of his nature, upholding the universe by his word of power. (Hebrews 1:1-3)

That which was from the beginning, which we have heard, which we have seen with our eyes, which we have looked upon and touched with our hands, concerning the word of life—the life was made manifest, and we saw it, and testify to it, and proclaim to you the eternal life which was with the Father and was made manifest to us. (1 John 1:1-2)

Treasuring the Word

A Reading from *Life of Jesus* by François Mauriac

End of the Hidden Life

The excitement raised by the preaching of John the Baptist reached Nazareth. . . . We can imagine, in his workshop there, the man waiting for his hour that was soon to come. Perhaps Mary spoke to him of John, of the son of her cousin Elizabeth and of his mysterious birth. . . .

The last days of the hidden life: the workman is no longer a workman; he refuses all orders and the workshop takes on an abandoned air. He had always prayed, but now day and night Mary would come upon him, his face against the earth. Perhaps he was already seized with impatience that all be accomplished, an impatience which he showed so often during the three years of his ascent to Calvary. How he longed to hear the first cracking of that fire he had come to light! Until that hour, God had so far sunk Himself in man that even his mother, although the mystery had been made known to her, had forgotten it, and allowed herself to rest beneath the weight of her crushing knowledge; he was her child, like other children whose brow she kissed, over whose sleep she watched; a young man whose tunic she mended. He earned his bread, seated himself at table to eat his meals, talked with the neighbors—and there was no lack of other artisans pious like himself and versed in the Scriptures. No doubt he was the same man who, during those last days, went to the door, listened with an absent expression and without comment to what the people said, but attentive to the rumours concerning John, now coming from every quarter. Already a power was manifesting itself in him which his mother alone was to see. Yes, a man, or rather "the man," he who was designated by the mysterious name "the Son of Man."

Already he was far away, his thought entirely on what he loved, on humanity which he must win—from what an enemy! . . . For Jesus was the light come into a world delivered over to the powers of darkness. . . .

At this moment of his life, the Son of Man was the gladiator still hidden in obscurity but about to enter the blinding arena—the fighter awaited and feared by the beast. "I beheld," Christ was to cry one day in exaltation, "I beheld Satan fall like a lightning-flash from heaven." It was perhaps during those last hours of the hidden life that he had the vision of that fall. Did he also see (and how could he not have seen!) that the vanquished archangel carried in his wake millions of souls, more numerous and thickly falling than the flakes of a snow storm?

He took a cloak, he tied on his sandals. To his mother he said words of farewell that we shall never know.

The Good News of the Kingdom

Jesus went about all Galilee, teaching in their synagogues and preaching the gospel of the kingdom and healing every disease and every infirmity among the people.
Matthew 4:23

Jesus alerts anyone who would listen to the fact that the victorious presence of God is at hand and that the death throes of creation and of history are about to come to an end.
Erasmo Leiva-Merikakis,
Fire of Mercy, Heart of the Word

With Healing in His Hands

He laid his hands on every one of them and healed them.

Search me through and through, O Lord.
Explore my sin-bruised being
and bind up my injuries
(whether gained through fault or folly).

As I surrender to your skilled hands and healing touch,
your fingers strip away my protections and self-illusions,
probing the wounds of my heart,
the raw sores of my soul,
my aching disappointments and mutilated hopes.
And then with patient care and Spirit's balm,
you nurse me back to sound wholeness in you,
restoring my vitality
and giving new exercise to my so-long-crippled love.

The Scene

[12]Now when [Jesus] heard that John had been arrested, he withdrew into Galilee; [13]and leaving Nazareth he went and dwelt in Capernaum by the sea, in the territory of Zebulun and Naphtali, that what was spoken by the prophet Isaiah might be fulfilled:

[15]   "The land of Zebulun and the land
            of Naphtali,
      toward the sea, across the Jordan,
      Galilee of the Gentiles—
[16]   the people who sat in darkness
      have seen a great light,
      and for those who sat in the region
            and shadow of death
      light has dawned."

[17]From that time Jesus began to preach, saying, "Repent, for the kingdom of heaven is at hand."

[23]And he went about all Galilee, teaching in their synagogues and preaching the gospel of the kingdom and healing every disease and every infirmity among the people. [24]So his fame spread throughout all Syria, and they brought him all the sick, those afflicted with various diseases and pains, demoniacs, epileptics, and paralytics, and he healed them. [25]And great crowds followed him from Galilee and the Decapolis and Jerusalem and Judea and from beyond the Jordan.

Luke 4:16-24, 28-32, 40-44
The Scene

[16]And [Jesus] came to Nazareth, where he had been brought up; and he went to the synagogue, as his custom was, on the sabbath day. And he stood up to read; [17]and there was given to him the book of the prophet Isaiah. He opened the book and found the place where it was written,

[18] "The Spirit of the Lord is upon me,
    because he has anointed me to preach
        good news to the poor.
    He has sent me to proclaim release to
        the captives
    and recovering of sight to the blind,
    to set at liberty those who are
        oppressed,
[19] to proclaim the acceptable year of
        the Lord."

[20]And he closed the book, and gave it back to the attendant, and sat down; and the eyes of all in the synagogue were fixed on him. [21]And he began to say to them, "Today this scripture has been fulfilled in your hearing." [22]And all spoke well of him, and wondered at the gracious words which proceeded out of his mouth; and they said, "Is not this Joseph's son?" [23]And he said to them, "Doubtless you will quote to me this proverb, 'Physician, heal yourself; what we have heard you did at Capernaum, do here also in your own country.'" [24]And he said, "Truly, I say to you, no prophet is acceptable in his own country." . . . [28]When they heard this, all in the synagogue were filled with wrath. [29]And they rose up and put him out of the city, and led him to the brow of the hill on which their city was built, that they might throw him down headlong. [30]But passing through the midst of them he went away.

[31]And he went down to Capernaum, a city of Galilee. And he was teaching them on the sabbath; [32]and they were astonished at his teaching, for his word was with authority.

[40]Now when the sun was setting, all those who had any that were sick with various diseases brought them to him; and he laid his hands on every one of them and healed them. [41]And demons also came out of many, crying, "You are the Son of God!" But he rebuked them, and would not allow them to speak, because they knew that he was the Christ.

[42]And when it was day he departed and went into a lonely place. And the people sought him and came to him, and would have kept him from leaving them; [43]but he said to them, "I must preach the good news of the kingdom of God to the other cities also; for I was sent for this purpose." [44]And he was preaching in the synagogues of Judea.

Reflecting on the Word

After his baptism, Jesus went to Capernaum, a fishing village on the northwest shore of Lake Gennesaret. From this home base, he taught and preached throughout Galilee (Matthew 4:12-13; Mark 2:1). Capernaum was located in the area settled by the tribes of Naphtali and Zebulun in the northern kingdom. This territory had been invaded and occupied by Assyria in 734 B.C. and was flooded with gentiles, while many of the Jewish population had been deported. When Jesus took up his ministry there, Isaiah's prophecy foretelling the exiles' deliverance was fulfilled:

> The land of Zebulun and the land of
>   Naphtali,
> toward the sea, across the Jordan,
> Galilee of the Gentiles—
> the people who sat in darkness
> have seen a great light,
> and for those who sat in the region
>   and shadow of death
> light has dawned. (Matthew 4:15-16;
> see also Isaiah 9:1-2)

Thus, this region, so despoiled in Isaiah's time, was the first to see the light of Christ dawning on it. "When Christ appeared in those lands . . . something began on earth like when a stone is cast into a quiet lake and starts ripples that finally reach the farthest shores," wrote Archbishop Oscar Romero. "Christ appeared in Zebulun and Naphtali with the signs of liberation: shaking off oppressive yokes, bringing joy to hearts, sowing hope. And this is what God is doing now in history" (*The Violence of Love*).

Jesus' first message echoed that of John the Baptist, "Repent, for the kingdom of heaven is at hand" (Matthew 4:17), and provided the bridge between the ministries of John the Baptist and Jesus. Commenting on Matthew's gospel, theologian Erasmo Leiva-Merikakis said Jesus chose those first words "to show his debt of gratitude to the Baptist and his strict continuity with him." However, "now the word of preparation becomes the word of fulfillment" (*Fire of Mercy, Heart of the Word*). As the herald faithfully completed his task, the Messiah began his own—and God's promises were thus being fully realized.

Both John and Jesus challenged their hearers to repentance and conversion of heart in order to receive the kingdom of God—that is, God's reign on earth, a reign exercised in the lives of men and women. However, whereas John's work had been to proclaim what would happen in the future and prepare the way for it, Jesus announced a kingdom that had arrived in its fullness and was present among his hearers. Jesus proclaimed "good news," thus personifying in himself Isaiah's prophecy,

> How beautiful upon the mountains
>   are the feet of him who brings
>   good tidings,
> who publishes peace, who brings

good tidings of good,
who publishes salvation,
who says to Zion, "Your God
    reigns."
    (52:7)

In his preaching and teaching—through sermons, exhortations, and parables—Jesus unfolded the values of God's kingdom and the principles of "kingdom living"—a kingdom often at odds with worldly values. It is a kingdom of priceless worth: "The kingdom of heaven is like treasure hidden in a field . . ." (Matthew 13:44). It starts out small but grows into something much bigger: "To what shall I compare the kingdom of God? It is like leaven . . ." (Luke 13:20-21). It requires great humility: "Unless you turn and become like children, you will never enter the kingdom of heaven" (Matthew 18:3). The kingdom that Jesus proclaimed is a kingdom where God reigns.

Matthew tells us that Jesus "went about all Galilee, teaching in their synagogues and preaching the gospel of the kingdom and healing every disease and every infirmity among the people. So his fame spread throughout all Syria, and they brought him all the sick, those afflicted with various diseases and pains, demoniacs, epileptics, and paralytics, and he healed them" (Matthew 4:23-24). This is a clear and concise summary of the works of the Messiah, which mirrored the messianic signs that had also been foretold by Isaiah:

Then the eyes of the blind shall be
    opened,
    and the ears of the deaf unstopped;
then shall the lame man leap like a
    hart,
    and the tongue of the dumb sing
    for joy.
    (35:5-6)

Indeed, these signs described by Isaiah were the answer that Jesus gave to the disciples of John the Baptist in reply to their inquiry, "Are you he who is to come, or shall we look for another?" (Matthew 11:2-5). The miracles and healings that Christ performed both affirmed and demonstrated that he had a God-given mission to bring salvation and the good news of God's kingdom to all who would believe.

Luke's account of Jesus' visit to his hometown of Nazareth further emphasizes the prophetic fulfillment of God's promises embodied in Jesus—the Christ, the anointed one. When Jesus came to the synagogue as was his custom, "there was given to him the book of the prophet Isaiah" (Luke 4:17). Finding these prophetic words, he read to his fellow townspeople:

The Spirit of the Lord is upon me,
because he has anointed me to preach
    good news to the poor.
He has sent me to proclaim release to
    the captives
and recovering of sight to the blind,

to set at liberty those who are
    oppressed,
to proclaim the acceptable year of
    the Lord.
(Luke 4:18-19; see also Isaiah 61:1-2)

Anointed by the Spirit at his baptism, Jesus took up the mission entrusted to him by the Father and now identified himself as the one foretold in Isaiah's prophecy, declaring, "Today this scripture has been fulfilled in your hearing" (Luke 4:21). This declaration was "followed by the actions and words known through the Gospel. By these actions and words Christ makes the Father present among men. . . . [T]he Messiah becomes a particularly clear sign of God who is love, a sign of the Father" (Pope John Paul II, *Rich in Mercy*).

The good news that Jesus proclaimed and the kingdom that he ushered in confounded the expectations of most of his hearers. The glory of King David and his descendants had been dimmed by their failures, sins, and defeats at the hands of their enemies. Israel longed for an heir to David's dynasty—an ideal ruler, a messianic figure—whom God would raise up to establish justice, build an empire, bring peace, and restore the throne of David. By Jesus' time, the messiah many Jews hoped for was a political leader who would free their nation from the domination of Rome.

Jesus' behavior and actions contradicted this understanding of a messianic ruler and transcended nationalistic conceptions of his role. Yet he seemed ambivalent about verbally declaring or clarifying his identity as the Messiah. On the one hand, Jesus did not deny that he was God's agent, sent by God to establish the new order that he was so openly proclaiming. When the woman at the well in Samaria said, "I know that Messiah is coming (he who is called Christ); when he comes, he will show us all things," Jesus replied, "I who speak to you am he" (John 4:25-26). And he accepted Peter's and Martha's professions of faith in him as "the Christ, the Son of the living God" (Matthew 16:16; John 11:27). On the other hand, however, Jesus did not want people to think of him as a political figure who would conquer Israel's enemies and establish a new Davidic kingdom on earth, a role he refused and rejected. So when his identity was being questioned, Jesus' responses were generally oblique: "You have said so" (Matthew 26:64; 27:11); "Why do you ask me?" (John 18:21) "If I tell you, you will not believe; and if I ask you, you will not answer" (Luke 22:66-68).

The Messiah—the Son of God, the Word-made-flesh—was sent into the world by the Father to redeem humankind from sin, liberate us from slavery to sin and death, and restore us to full union with God. Each of us must search our hearts to fully recognize our own need for a Messiah so that we can receive the salvation he offers us.

Pondering the Word

1. Note as many similarities as you can between John the Baptist's message and that of Jesus. What does this suggest to you? In what ways did their respective messages and missions differ?

_____

_____

_____

_____

_____

_____

_____

_____

_____

_____

2. Matthew and Luke stressed the fulfillment of Isaiah's prophecies as Jesus began to preach throughout Galilee and as he taught in the synagogue at Nazareth. How might Jesus' consciousness of his role and identity as the Messiah as described by Isaiah have affected his public ministry?

_____

_____

_____

_____

_____

_____

_____

_____

_____

3. Jesus proclaimed the gospel or good news of the kingdom (Matthew 4:23; Luke 4:43). What do you think a first-century Jew would have recognized as "good news" in the public ministry of Jesus? What good news might they think was lacking?

_____

_____

_____

_____

_____

_____

_____

_____

_____

4. What, in your opinion, did Jesus' hearers understand by his reading of Isaiah 61:1-2 in the synagogue in Nazareth? Why might they have reacted negatively to him (Luke 4:28)?

_____

_____

_____

_____

_____

_____

_____

_____

_____

5. Why would the demons have recognized the identity of Jesus when the religious people of the day did not (Luke 4:40-41)? Why do you think Jesus forbade the demons to speak when he rebuked them?

_____

_____

_____

_____

_____

_____

_____

_____

_____

6. Note all the geographical places listed in Matthew 4:12-13, 23-25. Relate this to Jesus' statement in Luke 4:43: "I must preach the good news of the kingdom of God to the other cities also." What do these two texts say about Jesus' call and mission?

_____

_____

_____

_____

_____

_____

_____

_____

_____

Living the Word

1. Picture yourself among the crowds that came to Jesus to be healed. How do you think you might have reacted? How easy or difficult is it for you to believe that Jesus still heals people today?

_____

_____

_____

_____

_____

_____

_____

_____

_____

2. What effect has the "good news" had on your daily life? On your world outlook? On your eternal perspective?

_____

_____

_____

_____

_____

_____

_____

_____

_____

3. What manifestations of the kingdom of God do you see around you? Would someone meeting you for the first time detect any signs or clues that you are living in God's kingdom? Why or why not?

_____

_____

_____

_____

_____

_____

_____

_____

_____

4. In what ways have you experienced the messianic activities of Jesus described in Isaiah 61:1-2 for yourself? Which of these actions speaks most directly to you at this time in your life?

_____

_____

_____

_____

_____

_____

_____

_____

_____

5. How are you actively sharing in Jesus' messianic work and mission? What are some concrete ways you can build God's kingdom in your home? In your workplace? In your parish?

_____

_____

_____

_____

_____

_____

_____

_____

_____

6. The Jewish people had different assumptions about what a messiah should do, and this prevented some of them from recognizing Jesus as the Messiah. How can our preconceptions and assumptions about how God acts in the world today keep us from recognizing his presence? Think of a time when you may have missed God's action in your life because you were expecting something else.

_____

_____

_____

_____

_____

_____

_____

_____

Rooted in the Word

Jesus: A Portrait of Redeeming Love

Sent by the Father for the salvation of the world, Jesus proclaimed the good news of the kingdom of God and brought healing and deliverance, comfort and reassurance, forgiveness of sin and new life. Through Jesus the Messiah, God's love was made visible and tangible to humankind. As Pope John Paul II wrote,

> Christ—the very fulfillment of the messianic prophecy—by becoming the incarnation of the love that is manifested with particular force with regard to the suffering, the unfortunate and sinners, makes present and thus more fully reveals the Father, who is God "rich in mercy." At the same time, by becoming for people a model of merciful love for others, Christ proclaims by His actions even more than by His words that call to mercy which is one of the essential elements of the Gospel ethos. (*Rich in Mercy*)

Jesus carried out his mission to the fullest, revealing to us the heart of the Father as well as the depth of his own love. Indeed, he died of love for us, pouring out his life on the cross to redeem us by his blood. "Greater love has no man than this, that a man lay down his life for his friends" (John 15:13).

Read and prayerfully reflect on these additional Scripture passages that portray Jesus' compassionate and redeeming love:

Jesus went about all the cities and villages, teaching in their synagogues and preaching the gospel of the kingdom, and healing every disease and every infirmity. When he saw the crowds, he had compassion for them, because they were harassed and helpless, like sheep without a shepherd.
(Matthew 9:35-36)

[T]hey brought to [Jesus] all who were sick or possessed with demons. And the whole city was gathered together about the door. And he healed many who were sick with various diseases, and cast out many demons; and he would not permit the demons to speak, because they knew him. And in the morning, a great while before day, he rose and went out to a lonely place, and there he prayed. And Simon and those who were with him followed him, and they found him and said to him, "Every one is searching for you." And he said to them, "Let us go on to the next towns, that I may preach there also; for that is why I came out." And he went throughout all Galilee, preaching in their synagogues and casting out demons. (Mark 1:32-39)

For God so loved the world that he gave his only Son, that whoever believes in him should not perish but have eternal life. For God sent the Son into the world, not to condemn the world, but that the world might be saved through him. (John 3:16-17)

God shows his love for us in that while we were yet sinners Christ died for us. Since, therefore, we are now justified by his blood, much more shall we be saved by him from the wrath of God. For if while we were enemies we were reconciled to God by the death of his Son, much more, now that we are reconciled, shall we be saved by his life. Not only so, but we also rejoice in God through our Lord Jesus Christ, through whom we have now received our reconciliation. (Romans 5:8-11)

In this the love of God was made manifest among us, that God sent his only Son into the world, so that we might live through him. In this is love, not that we loved God but that he loved us and sent his Son to be the expiation for our sins. (1 John 4:9-10)

Treasuring the Word

A Reading from *The Inner Life of Jesus* by Romano Guardini

How Christ Relieves Our Sufferings

Christ heals the sick. On the very first pages of the Gospels, He appears as the healer. He had hardly begun His teaching when the sick started coming. They were brought to Him from every quarter. It was as if the masses of the afflicted were always opening up around and closing in on Him. They came by themselves, they were led, they were carried, and He passed through the suffering multitude of people, and "a power from God was present, and healed" (Luke 5:17). . . .

At times, one is prompted to look behind the outward events at the inner working of this sacred power.

A blind man came to Him. Jesus put His hands on the man's eyes, drew them away, and asked, "What seest thou?" All overcome with excitement, the man answered, "I can see men as if they were trees, but walking!" The healing power reached into the nerves. They were revivified, but they did not yet work properly. So He put His hands on the eyes once again, and the man saw things as they were (Mark 8:23-25). Does not this story give one a sense of experiencing the mystery, as it were, from behind the scenes?

Another time, there was a great crowd about Him. A woman afflicted many years with a hemorrhage, who had sought everywhere in vain for a cure and had spent all her money to find one, said to herself, "If I can even touch His cloak, I shall be healed." And she came up to Him from behind, touched His garment, and noticed in her body that the distress which had been plaguing her for so long was at an end. But He turned around: "Who touched my garments?" The Apostles were dumbfounded: "Canst Thou see the multitude pressing so close about Thee, and yet ask, 'Who touched me?'" But He knew just what He was saying; immediately He had been "inwardly aware of the power that had proceeded from Him." And the woman came up to Him trembling, threw herself at His feet, and confessed what had happened. But He forgave her freely and lovingly (Mark 5:25-34; Luke 8:43-48).

What an effect that had all around! He seemed charged with healing, as if He needed no intention. If someone approached Him in an open-hearted, petitioning state of mind, the power simply proceeded from Him to do its work.

What did the act of healing mean to Christ? It has been said that He was the great friend of mankind. Characteristic of our own time is an extremely alert sense of social responsibility and responsiveness to works of mercy. So there has been a corresponding desire to see in Him the towering helper of men, who saw human suffering and, out of His great mercy, hastened to relieve it.

But this is an error. Jesus is not a personification of the big-hearted charitable nature with a great social conscience and an elemental power of helping others, going after human suffering, feeling its pangs in sympathy, understanding it, and conquering it. The social worker and the relief worker are trying to diminish suffering, to dispose of it entirely, if possible. Such a person hopes to have happy, healthy people, well-balanced in body and soul, live on this earth. We have to see this to understand that Jesus had no such thing in mind. It does not run counter to His wishes, but He Himself was not concerned with this. He saw too deeply into suffering. For the meaning of suffering, along with sin and estrangement from God, was to be found at the very roots of being. In the last analysis, suffering for Him represented the open road, the access back to God—at least the instrument which can serve as access. Suffering is a consequence of guilt, it is true, but at the same time, it is the means of purification and return.

We are much closer to the truth if we say Christ took the sufferings of mankind upon Himself. He did not recoil from them, as man always does. He did not overlook suffering. He did not protect Himself from it. He let it come to Him, took it into His heart. As far as suffering went, He accepted people as they were, in their true condition. He cast Himself in the midst of all the distress of mankind, with its guilt, want, and wretchedness.

This is a tremendous thing, a love of the greatest seriousness, no enchantments or illusions—and therefore, a love of overwhelming power because it is a "deed of truth in love" (Ephesians 4:15; 1 John 3:18), unbinding, shaking things to their roots.

Once again we must see the difference: He did this, not as one carrying on his shoulders the black tragedy of the human condition, but rather as one who was to comprehend it all, from God's point of view. Therein lies the characteristic distinction.

Christ's healing derives from God. It reveals God, and leads to God. . . . By healing, Jesus revealed Himself in action. Thus He gives concrete expression to the reality of the living God. To make men penetrate to the reality of the living God—that is why Christ healed.

Flashes of Glory

This is my Son, my Chosen; listen
to him!
Luke 9:35

Let us journey into the
    heavenly and holy mountain,
And let us gaze with our minds
    and hearts
At the spiritual Godhead of the
    Father and the Holy Spirit,
Shining forth in the only-
    begotten Son.
**Byzantine Hymn for the
Feast of the Transfiguration**

Eternity's Bright Vision

And he was transfigured before them,
and his face shone like the sun,
and his garments became white as light.

My frail and fragile frame cannot contain you yet, O Lord.
Seeing but your shadow takes away my breath
and a glimpse of your splendor overwhelms me,
your burning beauty engulfing me like fire.

More of you I cannot bear to see,
though my heart longs for that day
when I shall gaze upon you face to face.

And so I ask you:
Prepare me for eternity's bright vision.

Purify my eyes
that I might behold your unveiled glory.

Cleanse me of my sin
that I might stand upon your holy mountain.

And fortify my soul
that I might endure the full force of your radiance
and wholly satisfy the claims you make on me.

[18]Now it happened that as he was praying alone the disciples were with him; and he asked them, "Who do the people say that I am?" [19]And they answered, "John the Baptist; but others say, Elijah; and others, that one of the old prophets has risen." [20]And he said to them, "But who do you say that I am?" And Peter answered, "The Christ of God." [21]But he charged and commanded them to tell this to no one, [22]saying, "The Son of man must suffer many things, and be rejected by the elders and chief priests and scribes, and be killed, and on the third day be raised."

[23]And he said to all, "If any man would come after me, let him deny himself and take up his cross daily and follow me. [24]For whoever would save his life will lose it; and whoever loses his life for my sake, he will save it. [25]For what does it profit a man if he gains the whole world and loses or forfeits himself? [26]For whoever is ashamed of me and of my words, of him will the Son of man be ashamed when he comes in his glory and the glory of the Father and of the holy angels. [27]But I tell you truly, there are some standing here who will not taste death before they see the kingdom of God."

[28]Now about eight days after these sayings he took with him Peter and John and James, and went up on the mountain to pray. [29]And as he was praying, the appearance of his countenance was altered, and his raiment became dazzling white. [30]And behold, two men talked with him, Moses and Elijah, [31]who appeared in glory and spoke of his departure, which he was to accomplish at Jerusalem. [32]Now Peter and those who were with him were heavy with sleep but kept awake, and they saw his glory and the two men who stood with him. [33]And as the men were parting from him, Peter said to Jesus, "Master, it is well that we are here; let us make three booths, one for you and one for Moses and one for Elijah"—not knowing what he said. [34]As he said this, a cloud came and overshadowed them; and they were afraid as they entered the cloud. [35]And a voice came out of the cloud, saying, "This is my Son, my Chosen; listen to him!" [36]And when the voice had spoken, Jesus was found alone. And they kept silence and told no one in those days anything of what they had seen.

See also Matthew 16:13-21, 24-28; 17:1-8; Mark 8:27-31, 34-38; 9:2-10

Reflecting on the Word

The disciples had been in Jesus' company for months on end. Yet it must have been clear to Jesus that they still did not understand him and the mission that his Father had sent him to accomplish. Jesus was ready to question them directly. In doing so, he would reveal his true identity.

First he asked them about the people who so eagerly gathered to hear him: Who did they think he was? The disciples offered some of the popular notions that were circulating about his identity. Not satisfied to hear only the opinions of the crowds, Jesus probed further. He wanted to know what his closest followers made of him. Were their hearts dull and their eyes blind like so many others who failed to recognize his true identity? Surely the disciples had often discussed this question among themselves, not daring to ask Jesus himself. Now he pressed the crucial question home to his own circle of friends: "Who do you say that I am?" Simon Peter, spokesman for the group, boldly replied: "The Christ of God" (Luke 9:18-20).

Jesus knew that Peter's answer could only have been prompted by divine revelation: "Blessed are you, Simon Bar-Jona! For flesh and blood has not revealed this to you, but my Father who is in heaven" (Matthew 16:17). Scripture commentator Alfred MacBride notes how Peter's response surpassed his human understanding and perception:

The richness of Peter's answer is dazzling. In the light of God's fire, he speaks as though uttering an oracle. The words form on his lips, not like the easy declaration of logic, let alone the subtle conclusion of inductive reasoning. . . . What neither the religious learning of the pharisees, the peasant cunning of the people nor the sheer intimacy of the apostleship could discern, Peter is the first to see. His words are not the result of cold calculations, ignorant superstition or flattery. He is far too innocent to resort to such tactics.

Peter's words are born in ecstasy. The blunt fisherman has become a spiritual oracle because the Holy Spirit has taken hold of his heart and offered his mind that luminous insight. (*The Kingdom and the Glory: Meditation and Commentary on the Gospel of Matthew*)

In declaring Jesus as the Christ, Simon Peter and the disciples probably hoped that he would deliver Israel from its enemies. Although Peter had been inspired by God, his human comprehension was limited. Just a short time after his inspired proclamation of faith, Peter railed against Jesus' predictions of his sufferings and death, not realizing that only in this way could Jesus fulfill God's true definition of the Messiah (Matthew 16:21-22). Jesus was already familiar with Satan's efforts to deflect him from God's call (Luke 4:1-13). So now he recognized this new attempt, in the guise of a friend's concern, and rebuked Peter as Satan's instrument (Matthew 16:23).

It is noteworthy that Jesus did not count Peter's shortsightedness against him. He still chose the man whom he described as "not on the side of God, but of men" (Matthew 16:23) to be the rock on which he would establish his church (16:18). God chooses to use us as partners in accomplishing his purposes, even when we seem to show little understanding of what they are!

Peter's confession marks a turning point in the gospels. After it, Jesus—often referring to himself as "the Son of man"—began to speak openly with his disciples about his coming passion (Matthew 16:21; 17:22-23; Mark 8:31; 9:31; 10:33-34; Luke 9:21-22, 43-45). The Hebrew Scriptures use the term "son of man" frequently as a synonym for a member of the human race, that is, a son of Adam, stressing our frail human condition and littleness before God (Job 25:6; Psalms 8:4; 80:17; Ezekiel 2:1, 3). By calling himself the Son of man, Jesus identified himself as a human being like us—but without any of the weaknesses of sinful humanity. The prophet Daniel used the title in an apocalyptic sense, vividly foretelling the coming of the Son of man in glory, ushering in his kingdom: "[B]ehold, with the clouds of heaven there came one like a son of man. . . . And to him was given dominion and

glory and kingdom" (Daniel 7:13-14). In a similar vein, Jesus spoke of his final coming: "The Son of man is to come with his angels in the glory of his Father" (Matthew 16:27; see also Mark 13:24-27).

The vital question "Who do you say I am?" required a personal commitment from each of Jesus' disciples—a commitment required of each of us, too. And this faith response to Jesus the Messiah also demands a response to his call to radical discipleship: "If any man would come after me, let him deny himself and take up his cross daily and follow me" (Luke 9:23).

Jesus' mysterious transfiguration took place shortly after Peter's profession of faith and Jesus' first prophecy of his death. Jesus went up to a high mountain to pray and took his three closest friends with him. "Then something happened to him; perhaps it had happened before, but this time they were there to see it. In some way his longing love burst the barriers between mortality and immortality. . . . The apostles saw the radiant Lord of life, as he would be when death was conquered" (Maria Boulding, *The Coming of God*).

Did Jesus allow Peter, James, and John to glimpse his glory so that they would be able to bear the adversities and dark times to come with greater fortitude? "The great reason for this transfiguration," St. Leo the Great suggested, "was to remove the scandal of the cross from the hearts of his disciples, and to prevent the humiliation of his voluntary suffering from disturbing the faith of those who had witnessed the surpassing glory that lay concealed" (*Sermon 51*).

Surely the memory of those moments with Jesus on the mountain must have comforted the bewildered apostles as they grieved after Jesus' death—and later strengthened them as they passed through other difficult moments in their lives. Years afterward, Peter still vividly recalled this profound experience, writing to his fellow Christians, "We were eyewitnesses of his majesty . . . for we were with him on the holy mountain" (2 Peter 1:16-18).

Peter, James, and John were weary after the long ascent up the mountain. In spite of their fatigue, they "kept awake" as Jesus prayed—and were blessed to see his transfiguration (Luke 9:32). We too must struggle against falling spiritually "asleep" so we don't miss those "flashes of God's glory," as author Louise Perrotta calls them, which shine "into our ordinary surroundings." While they may not be as spectacular as Jesus' radiance on the mountain, they are "little transfigurations that God offers to anyone who is 'fully awake' to their transforming potential" (*2004: A Book of Grace-Filled Days*).

Moses and Elijah, representing the law and the prophets, appeared as witnesses to Jesus as the Messiah, the fulfillment of all they had taught and foretold. Luke tells us that they spoke with Jesus of his "departure"—that is, his "exodus"—that

he was going to accomplish in Jerusalem (Luke 9:31). This exodus calls to mind the Israelites' deliverance from Egypt—which was a prefigurement of the salvation Jesus won for us through his death, resurrection, and ascension.

"And as the men were departing from him, Peter said to Jesus, 'Master, it is well that we are here; let us make three booths, one for you and one for Moses and one for Elijah'—not knowing what he said" (Luke 9:33). The glory of this scene was so great that it overwhelmed and confused the apostles, although Peter realized that it was a moment of special importance and sought to prolong it.

In many ways Jesus' transfiguration parallels Yahweh's manifestation to Moses on Mount Sinai and the experience of the Israelites who similarly witnessed the glory of God and heard the voice at the mountain (Deuteronomy 5:4, Exodus 24:13, 15). Like these Old Testament prototypes, the transfiguration occurred on a mountain (Luke 9:28). Both Jesus and Moses took three companions with them (Luke 9:28; Exodus 24:1), and the faces of both shone with God's glory (Matthew 17:2, Exodus 34:29). Each of these manifestations of God also included a cloud indicating his presence as well as the heavenly voice (Luke 9:35; Exodus 24:16; Deuteronomy 4:12; 5:22-24).

The Father's voice, the chosen Son, and the cloud of the Spirit reveal the presence of the Trinity. The Father's words—"This is my Son, my Chosen" (Luke 9:35)—announce Jesus' divine sonship and echo Isaiah 42, where the Lord's chosen servant is empowered by the Spirit to bring relief to the oppressed and justice to all nations (42:1-7). "Listen to him" recalls Deuteronomy 18:15, Moses' prophecy that another prophet like himself would someday arise in Israel, and "him you shall heed." Thus, Jesus, whose teaching is backed by the approval and authority of the Father, is to be followed as the Israelites had earlier followed Moses.

Summarizing this extraordinary event and the powerful force it still exerts on us today, the late Pope John Paul II wrote,

The Gospel scene of Christ's transfiguration, in which the three Apostles Peter, James and John appear entranced by the beauty of the Redeem-er, can be seen as an icon of Christian contemplation. To look upon the face of Christ, to recognize its mystery amid the daily events and the sufferings of his human life, and then to grasp the divine splendor definitively revealed in the Risen Lord, seated in glory at the right hand of the Father: this is the task of each one of us. In contemplating Christ's face we become open to receiving the mystery of Trinitarian life, experiencing ever anew the love of the Father and delighting in the joy of the Holy Spirit. St. Paul's words can then be applied to us: "Beholding the glory of the Lord, we are being changed into his likeness, from one degree of glory to another; for this comes from the Lord who is the Spirit" (2 Corinthians 3:18). (*On the Most Holy Rosary*)

Pondering the Word

1. Peter, inspired by God, professed faith in Jesus as the Messiah, yet he still failed to completely understand what this meant. How and why, in your opinion, could belief and misunderstanding coexist in Peter at the same time? What does this indicate to you about Peter's character? About faith and intellectual understanding?

_____

_____

_____

_____

_____

_____

_____

_____

_____

_____

2. What do you think were Jesus' reasons for telling his disciples of his impending passion and death (Luke 9:22)? Why did Jesus choose this particular moment to speak openly to them of his coming sufferings? Why do you think Jesus commanded his disciples to say nothing to others of who he was and of the things he had told them (9:21)?

_____

_____

_____

_____

_____

_____

_____

_____

_____

_____

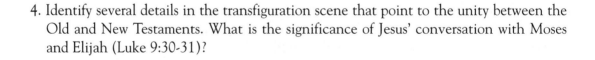

3. Jesus was at prayer when he asked the disciples, "Who do the people say that I am?" (Luke 9:18) and also when he was transfigured (9:29). What does this suggest to you about Jesus' prayer and his relationship with the Father? About your own prayer and your understanding of who Jesus is?

---

4. Identify several details in the transfiguration scene that point to the unity between the Old and New Testaments. What is the significance of Jesus' conversation with Moses and Elijah (Luke 9:30-31)?

---

5. In what ways do you think the transfiguration was meaningful for Jesus himself? For Peter, James, and John?

_____

_____

_____

_____

_____

_____

_____

_____

_____

6. What was the purpose of the manifestation of the cloud and heavenly voice at Jesus' transfiguration? At Jesus' baptism, a voice from heaven—that is, God the Father—had called Jesus "my beloved Son" (Matthew 3:17; Mark 1:11; Luke 3:22). Why do you think the voice from the cloud at the transfiguration added the injunction "Listen to him" (Luke 9:35)?

_____

_____

_____

_____

_____

_____

_____

_____

_____

Living the Word

1. Recall an instance when God may have used you in spite of your limited understanding of him and of his ways. What part did faith play in the situation?

_____

_____

_____

_____

_____

_____

_____

_____

_____

_____

2. How can misconceptions about Jesus and how he "ought" to act be an obstacle to your growth in faith? Write a prayer to Jesus, answering the question "Who do you say that I am?" and professing your faith in him.

_____

_____

_____

_____

_____

_____

_____

_____

_____

_____

3. Think of a time when you caught a glimpse of God's glory breaking through in the midst of a difficult situation. What effect did this have on you? How can the hope of the resurrection and heaven strengthen you on your earthly journey?

_____

_____

_____

_____

_____

_____

_____

_____

_____

4. Are there any areas of your life in which you are spiritually lethargic? How can you "wake up" and be more alert to God's presence in your life? To his will for you?

_____

_____

_____

_____

_____

_____

_____

_____

_____

5. The Father affirmed Jesus as his Chosen, his beloved Son. In what ways do you experience being the beloved of God? Are there any attitudes or experiences that make it difficult for you to believe you are God's beloved son or daughter?

_____

_____

_____

_____

_____

_____

_____

_____

_____

_____

6. The heavenly voice told Peter, James, and John to listen to Jesus (Luke 9:35). How is listening related to obeying? How do you "listen" to Jesus?

_____

_____

_____

_____

_____

_____

_____

_____

_____

_____

Rooted in the Word

Jesus: A Portrait of Glory

This dazzling glory revealed at Jesus' transfiguration was an expression of his divine nature and, as Archbishop Fulton Sheen so eloquently put it, "of the inherent loveliness of 'Him who came down from heaven.' The wonder was not this momentary radiance around Him; it was rather that at all other times it was repressed" (*Life of Christ*).

The brilliant light that so awed the apostles on the mountain of the transfiguration did not shine on Jesus from outside but radiated from within him, thoroughly altering the appearance of his countenance and his clothing as he prayed (Luke 9:29). Jesus' glory was unveiled to Peter, James, and John as he took on for a few moments the appearance that would be his throughout eternity. The transfiguration was a foretaste of the glorification of Christ's resurrected body, a hint of the glory that was to be his when, after the ascension, he took his seat at the Father's right hand. Not only did the transfiguration foreshadow the contemplation of God in eternity, where the blessed behold God's glory and beauty forever, it is also an anticipation of our own glorification and the destiny that is to be ours in Christ. "[W]e know that when he appears we shall be like him, for we shall see him as he is" (1 John 3:2).

Read and prayerfully reflect on these additional Scripture passages describing the glory of God and of Christ and the glory that we too are to share in:

[Daniel said:] "I saw in the night visions,
and behold, with the clouds of
    heaven
    there came one like a son of man,
and he came to the Ancient of Days
    and was presented before him.
And to him was given dominion
    and glory and kingdom,
that all peoples, nations, and
    languages
    should serve him;
his dominion is an everlasting
    dominion,
    which shall not pass away,
and his kingdom one
    that shall not be destroyed."
(Daniel 7:13-14)

[T]he high priest said to [Jesus], "I adjure you by the living God, tell us if you are the Christ, the Son of God." Jesus said to him, "You have said so. But I tell you, hereafter you will see the Son of man seated at the right hand of Power, and coming on the clouds of heaven." (Matthew 26:63-64)

Just as we have borne the image of the man of dust, we shall also bear the image of the man of heaven. I tell you this, brethren: flesh and blood cannot inherit the kingdom of God, nor does the perishable inherit the imperishable. Lo! I tell you a mystery. We shall not all sleep, but we shall all be changed, in a moment, in the twinkling of an eye, at the last trumpet. For the trumpet will sound, and the dead will be raised imperishable, and we shall be changed. For this perishable nature must put on the imperishable, and this mortal nature must put on immortality. (1 Corinthians 15:49-53)

[O]ur commonwealth is in heaven, and from it we await a Savior, the Lord Jesus Christ, who will change our lowly body to be like his glorious body, by the power which enables him even to subject all things to himself. (Philippians 3:20-21)

Then I [John] turned to see the voice that was speaking to me, and on turning I saw seven golden lampstands, and in the midst of the lampstands one like a son of man, clothed with a long robe and with a golden girdle round his breast; his head and his hair were white as white wool, white as snow; his eyes were like a flame of fire, his feet were like burnished bronze, refined as in a furnace, and his voice was like the sound of many waters; in his right hand he held seven stars, from his mouth issued a sharp two-edged sword, and his face was like the sun shining in full strength. When I saw him, I fell at his feet as though dead. But he laid his right hand upon me, saying, "Fear not, I am the first and the last, and the living one; I died, and behold I am alive for evermore, and I have the keys of Death and Hades." (Revelation 1:12-18)

Treasuring the Word

A Reading from a Homily by Karl Rahner, SJ
Given on the Feast of the Transfiguration, August 6, 1933

The Transfiguration of the Lord

The life of Jesus should be an example and a warning to us. But to understand what the mysteries of Christ's life want to say to us, we must know what they mean for Jesus himself. And so we inquire what place the transfiguration assumes in the life of the savior.

To understand this we need to consider that Jesus also had a human heart susceptible to joy and sorrow, pain and consolation; a heart that in a completely sinless, holy manner, but still really, experienced the changes wrought by all these storms of the soul as we do. The Son of God assumed indeed a true human nature with body and soul; he became like us in all things except sin. And so he could also be like us in that there was a place in his soul for the stirring of the mind, for the changes of joy and sadness, jubilation and lamentation.

As St. Augustine says: "In him who had a true human body and a true human soul, also the human emotions were not untrue." And really, if we page through the Gospels, then we discover how Jesus wept, then became happy again; how he looked upon one full of love, and upon others scornfully and with deep sadness; how he wondered at and enjoyed the one, sighed over others; how he was filled with joy, with zeal, stirred by compassion, shaken unto death, and deceived.

If we want to get a sense of what was going on in the heart of Jesus as he climbed the mount of transfiguration, then we have to take into account in what period in Jesus' life the transfiguration was. The savior had already preached a good deal in Judea and Galilee; he had proclaimed that the kingdom of God had come, had taught how people were supposed to receive it, had stated clearly enough that he is the promised messiah and the true Son of God. He came unto his own and his own received him not.

To be sure, he had a troop of loyal, if also imperfect, disciples and apostles, but the people as a whole had not believed. In Judea, where the Pharisees prevailed, there was a mishap right at the start. In Galilee, to be sure, the enthusiasm was great at the start, but it soon dissipated. The people sought miracles and bread more than faith. After the eucharistic discourse, even some of the disciples became disloyal. Pharisees and Sadducees worked against him now in Galilee as well, and always asked unbelievingly for new signs. And when Jesus asked, "Whom do the people say that I am?" the best appraisal made of him was that of a prophet. So Jesus' invitation to faith in him fell on deaf ears; the people had actually rejected its messiah already. There still remains only one thing: suffering and the cross. And so six days before the transfiguration, Jesus had predicted for the first time to the apostles his passion and death.

Now we can get some sense of the sort of thoughts and feelings that might surely have filled the heart of the savior as, with his three chosen apostles, in the quiet of the evening he climbed a lone high mountain far from all people and their busy noise. It will surely have been the feeling of pain over the ingratitude, hardheartedness, and unbelief of his people, thoughts of his coming passion, readiness and resolve for the cross, but also the anxiety and sadness of the Mount of Olives.

What does Jesus, in this mood of the holiest of hearts, then do? He prays. He goes away from human beings, he climbs a high mountain in order to hold converse, there in the quiet solitude of the mountain, in the restfulness of the long nights, with his Father in heaven, with his God, in whom that fate is meaningful, in whom even a defeat becomes a victory. Jesus loved these nights of prayer that bring human beings, their decisions and their fate before the

face of the eternal one. We read of these nights of prayer before the selection of the apostles, after the many miracles of healing in Capernaum, after the first multiplication of loaves of bread. So Jesus prayed also in this mood at this period in his life. There he will have prayed to the Father for his unbelieving people, for his apostles and disciples for faith and strength in the coming days of suffering. He will have said to his Father: See, I come to do your will. I am ready to drink the cup, to be baptized with the baptism of suffering. Yes, it presses down upon me, until it is accomplished.

No one goes unheard before the face of God. The Father hears the pleas of his much beloved Son. Union with God, which Jesus otherwise holds hidden in the ultimate depths of his soul, now fills up all the chambers of his soul, it embraces his body, drawing it, too, into the blessedness of God's light and God's unity. "His face was like the sun, and his clothes were as radiant as light." And still more: there appeared to him Moses and Elijah, the great proclaimer of the law and the prophets. And Jesus in between them as a sign that the law and the prophets have their goal and fulfillment; as a sign that he gives the power of fulfilling the law from within; that he is the wellspring and the plentitude of every Spirit at work in the prophets and presently to be poured forth upon all who believe in him. And because all redemption and all Holy Spirit takes its departure from the cross, they talk with Jesus about the leave taking he is supposed to set forth upon in Jerusalem. And just as at the baptism, the voice of the Father confirms here, too, that this poor, praying Jesus, consecrated for suffering, and heroically prepared for the cross, is God's very beloved Son.

This then is the meaning of the transfiguration for Jesus himself: in the dark night of earthly hopelessness the light of God shines, a human heart finds in God the power which turns a dying into a victory and into the redemption of the world.

"Hosanna to the Son of David!"

Lo, your king comes to you;
    triumphant and victorious is he,
humble and riding on an ass.
Zechariah 9:9

Jesus' entry into Jerusalem manifests
the coming of the kingdom that
the Messiah-King, welcomed into
his city by children and the humble
of heart, is going to accomplish
by the Passover of his Death and
Resurrection.
Catechism of the Catholic Church, 570

What Greeting for the King?

Jubilant *Hosannas*
(alive with hope and expectation)
resounded upon the fresh spring air
to welcome the king who
entered Jerusalem's walls that day
astride a donkey.

But soon his bleeding feet
will trip over the same rough paving stones
that had echoed his praises,
and hammer blows will rend the stagnant air
thick with dust and the smell of sweat and blood.
Only cries of mockery
(and mourning)
will greet Israel's king
when he's hung high upon a cross
outside the city walls,
all *Hosannas* dying
with this strange Messiah.

[1]And when they drew near to Jerusalem and came to Bethphage, to the Mount of Olives, then Jesus sent two disciples, [2]saying to them, "Go into the village opposite you, and immediately you will find an ass tied, and a colt with her; untie them and bring them to me. [3]If any one says anything to you, you shall say, 'The Lord has need of them,' and he will send them immediately." [4]This took place to fulfil what was spoken by the prophet, saying,

5   "Tell the daughter of Zion,
      Behold, your king is coming to you,
      humble, and mounted on an ass,
      and on a colt, the foal of an ass."

[6]The disciples went and did as Jesus had directed them; [7]they brought the ass and the colt, and put their garments on them, and he sat thereon. [8]Most of the crowd spread their garments on the road, and others cut branches from the trees and spread them on the road. [9]And the crowds that went before him and that followed him shouted, "Hosanna to the Son of David! Blessed is he who comes in the name of the Lord! Hosanna in the highest!" [10]And when he entered Jerusalem, all the city was stirred, saying, "Who is this?" [11]And the crowds said, "This is the prophet Jesus from Nazareth of Galilee."

[12]And Jesus entered the temple of God and drove out all who sold and bought in the temple, and he overturned the tables of the money-changers and the seats of those who sold pigeons. [13]He said to them, "It is written, 'My house shall be called a house of prayer'; but you make it a den of robbers."

[14]And the blind and the lame came to him in the temple, and he healed them. [15]But when the chief priests and the scribes saw the wonderful things that he did, and the children crying out in the temple, "Hosanna to the Son of David!" they were indignant; [16]and they said to him, "Do you hear what these are saying?" And Jesus said to them, "Yes; have you never read,

      'Out of the mouth of babes and
          sucklings
      thou hast brought perfect praise'?"

[17]And leaving them, he went out of the city to Bethany and lodged there.

**See also Mark 11:1-11, 15-19;
Luke 19:29-40, 45-48;
John 2:13-22**

Reflecting on the Word

Jesus had raised Lazarus from the dead, and so he was a man with a price on his head. He went into temporary seclusion (John 11:53-57), where he was refreshed by a visit with his friends and anointed beforehand for his burial (12:1-8). Jesus was now ready to enter Jerusalem openly, knowing he would confront its hostile authorities. He was approaching the culmination of his mission.

"Although Jesus had always refused popular attempts to make him king, he chooses the time and prepares the details for his messianic entry into the city of 'his father David'" (*Catechism of the Catholic Church*, 559). His entrance into Jerusalem on the Sunday before Passover was deliberate and purposeful, for it was popularly believed that the Messiah would come at Passover time to announce the establishment of his kingdom. Moreover, Jesus made special arrangements to ride into the city rather than walk as pilgrims usually did. A donkey awaited him, "tied at the door out in the open street" for his disciples to fetch (Mark 11:4). Jesus' choice of mount was symbolic as well as intentional, for his entrance into David's city on a donkey enacted ancient prophecies about the coming of Israel's Messiah-King:

> Say to the daughter of Zion,
> "Behold, your salvation comes."
> (Isaiah 62:11)

> Lo, your king comes to you;
> triumphant and victorious is he,

> humble and riding on an ass,
> on a colt the foal of an ass.
> (Zechariah 9:9)

In fulfilling these messianic prophecies, Jesus was publicly proclaiming his identity.

Jesus' manner of entering the city would have also recalled to the crowds the occasion when Solomon, King David's son, rode his father's mule from the site of his anointing at the spring of Gihon into Jerusalem, where he was crowned as David's successor to the throne (1 Kings 1:32-40). Now Jesus was greeted with a great crowd hailing him as "Son of David" and celebrating his kingship (Matthew 21:9).

Jesus rode a colt "on which no one has ever yet sat" (Luke 19:30). Animals that had not been yoked or broken for common use were ritually clean; since this colt filled the Old Testament prescriptions (see Numbers 19:2 and 1 Samuel 6:7), it was suitable for sacred or royal use.

As the crowds cheered, they spread their cloaks on the ground in Jesus' path, perhaps remembering how garments had been spread under Jehu's feet when he was hailed as king after he had been anointed by Elisha (2 Kings 9:13). Reflecting on this Palm Sunday scene centuries later, St. Andrew of Crete wrote,

> Let us run to accompany him as he
> hastens toward his passion. . . . [L]et
> us spread before his feet, not garments

. . . but ourselves, clothed in his grace, or rather, clothed completely in him. We who have been baptized into Christ must ourselves be the garments that we spread before him.

"Hosanna to the Son of David!" (Matthew 21:9) cried the crowds enthusiastically, lauding Jesus as subjects laud their king and praising him for the great works and miracles they had seen him perform (Luke 19:37). "Hosanna" is the Greek form of the Hebrew entreaty *hosa na*, meaning "Save (us), we beseech you" (see Psalm 118:25-26; 2 Samuel 14:4). Originally a cry for help, over time it became an invocation of blessing and even an acclamation of praise. In the Sanctus of the eucharistic liturgy, the church has taken up the crowd's cry: "Blessed is he who comes in the name of the Lord! Hosanna in the highest!" (Matthew 21:9). So we proclaim the kingship of Christ each time the memorial of Christ's Passover is celebrated.

Jesus willingly accepted the crowd's acclaim—but he still rejected the kind of kingship they envisioned. Fired with nationalism, many Jews looked for a warrior-king who would deliver them from Roman domination. But Jesus did not come on a warhorse to establish an independent Jewish state. He came on a mission of peace, astride a young ass. The crowds understood his kingship no better than the disciples did (John 12:16).

While Jesus made it clear that he did not come as a political king or liberator, he still claimed the honor and praise that belonged to him. He refused to quiet his followers when the Pharisees were scandalized by their messianic acclamations. "If these were silent," Jesus told the infuriated Pharisees, "the very stones would cry out" (Luke 19:39-40). "So obvious is his messiahship that if men refused to recognize it, nature would proclaim it. In fact, when his friends were cowed on the hill of Calvary the earth trembled and the rocks split [Matthew 27:51]" (*The Navarre Bible: The Gospel of Saint Luke*).

Many biblical scholars believe that Psalm 118 depicts a celebration in the temple of a king's victory. The crowds welcomed Jesus with a festal procession, palm branches, and the cry, "Hosanna! Blessed is he who come in the name of the Lord, even the King of Israel!" (John 12:13; see also Psalm 118:25-27). So they may have expected that he would enter the temple with the words, "Open to me the gates of righteousness" (Psalm 118:19), and declare his kingship at the altar.

In Matthew's chronology, Jesus did proceed immediately to the temple when he had entered Jerusalem from the Mount of Olives. But there he behaved quite unexpectedly, driving out all who bought and sold sacrificial animals and overturning the tables of the money changers (Matthew 21:12).

Selling animals and exchanging foreign currency were necessary services provided for Passover pilgrims who came to Jerusalem to offer sacrifice and pay the annual temple tax.

In fact, there were already four marketplaces selling sacrificial animals that were approved by the Sanhedrin, which were conveniently located in the area near the Mount of Olives. But under the high priest Caiaphas, the court of the gentiles, the outermost precinct of the temple, had also been turned into a trading place—an abuse that hindered gentile worshippers from praying there.

By evicting the traders, Jesus was defending God's intention that *all* people could worship at the temple, gentiles as well as Jews. For God had said,

[T]he foreigners who join themselves
     to the LORD,
  to minister to him, to love the
     name of the LORD,
  and to be his servants, . . .
these I will bring to my holy
     mountain,
  and make them joyful in my
     house of prayer . . .
for my house shall be called a house
     of prayer
  for all peoples. (Isaiah 56:6-7)

It is likely that, in addition to wanting to preserve the temple as a place of prayer, Jesus was disturbed by the corruption and excessive desire for gain that had come to surround the commercial activities carried out in the temple precinct. Pilgrims were exploited by money changers who charged an inflated rate of exchange and by merchants who sold animals for exorbitant prices. Such practices, Jesus declared quoting Jeremiah 7:11, made the temple into "a den of robbers" (Matthew 21:13). Perhaps he also intended his actions to be a reminder to the dealers that "You cannot serve God and mammon" (Luke 16:13).

The expulsion of the merchants from the temple is a fulfillment of the prophet Zechariah's vision of the messianic age: "There shall no longer be a trader in the house of the LORD of hosts on that day" (14:21). It also provided a hint that the sacrificial system, which was at the heart of Judaism, was about to become obsolete. An eternal sacrifice—Jesus' death and resurrection—would supersede the burnt sacrifices that had been offered constantly in the temple for so long. In fact, when the Jerusalem temple was destroyed by the Romans in A.D. 70, the practice of sacrificing animals ended.

After Jesus had expelled the merchants and money changers, "the blind and lame came to him in the temple, and he healed them" (Matthew 21:14). This description of the messianic works Jesus performed is a familiar refrain heard throughout gospels: "[A]ll those who had any that were sick with various diseases brought them to him; and he laid his hands on every one of them and healed them" (Luke 4:40). In it we also hear echoes of Isaiah 35:4-6, that "the eyes of the blind shall be opened, and . . . then shall the lame man leap like a hart," and Jesus' reply to John the Baptist's disciples, "Go and tell John what you hear and see: the blind receive their sight and the lame walk. . . . And blessed is he who takes no offense at me" (Matthew 11:4, 6).

But some did take offense at Jesus: The chief priests and scribes were indignant when they saw the wonders Jesus did and heard the praise the children gave him (Matthew 21:15). Jesus quoted Psalm 8:2 to them in reply: "Out of the mouth of babes and sucklings thou hast brought perfect praise." With this reference to infants glorifying the Lord, Jesus was giving another hint—this time of his divinity.

Those who controlled the temple commerce and profited from it—among them perhaps Caiaphas, his father-in-law, Annas, and their families—were angered by the disruption of business when Jesus cleansed the temple. Moreover, they feared Jesus, because the people listened attentively to him. After Jesus cleared out the temple, they sought a way to put him to death (Mark 11:17-18; Luke 19:45-47). Plans unfolded quickly:

Then the chief priests and the elders of the people gathered in the palace of the high priest, who was called Caiaphas, and took counsel together in order to arrest Jesus by stealth and kill him. . . . Then one of the twelve, who was called Judas Iscariot, went to the chief priests and said, "What will you give me if I deliver him to you?" And they paid him thirty pieces of silver. And from that moment he sought an opportunity to betray him. (Matthew 26:3-4, 14-16)

Pondering the Word

1. How do Jesus' preparations and entrance into Jerusalem add to your understanding of his messianic role? Why do you think it was important for him to make such an entrance?

_____

_____

_____

_____

_____

_____

_____

_____

_____

_____

2. What adjectives would you use to characterize the attitude and mood of the crowd as Jesus entered Jerusalem? What might this indicate about the crowd's expectations of him?

_____

_____

_____

_____

_____

_____

_____

_____

_____

3. What clues does Matthew give about how Jesus responded to the crowd's acclamation? How do you think Jesus' disciples might have felt as they watched their master?

_____

_____

_____

_____

_____

_____

_____

_____

_____

_____

4. What statement about himself and his mission was Jesus making by the cleansing of the temple? What does the presence of the blind and lame and children in the temple signify?

_____

_____

_____

_____

_____

_____

_____

_____

_____

_____

5. Why, in your opinion, were the chief priests and scribes so indignant toward Jesus (Matthew 21:15-16)? Is their reaction surprising to you? Why or why not?

_____

_____

_____

_____

_____

_____

_____

_____

_____

_____

6. Why did Jesus compare himself and his own body to the temple (Matthew 26:61; 27:40; Mark 14:58; John 2:20-22)? How has Jesus' sacrificial death replaced the temple sacrifice (Hebrews 9:11-14; 10:11-14)?

_____

_____

_____

_____

_____

_____

_____

_____

_____

_____

Living the Word

1. The Pharisees were hard-hearted in their view of Jesus, refusing to consider that he might truly be the Messiah. Recall a time when your hard-heartedness caused you to miss God's presence and action in your life. When did you recognize the need to repent?

_____

_____

_____

_____

_____

_____

_____

_____

_____

_____

2. What is your reaction to public expressions of devotion to the Lord? How free and open are you in expressing your love for Jesus and your commitment to him in front of others?

_____

_____

_____

_____

_____

_____

_____

_____

_____

_____

3. Is the description of Jesus' actions in the temple surprising to you? Disturbing? Why or why not? Has this scene altered your conception or expectations of Jesus in any way? If so, how?

_____

_____

_____

_____

_____

_____

_____

_____

_____

_____

4. Zeal for his Father's house consumed Jesus when he cleansed the temple (John 2:17; see also Psalm 69:9). To what do you zealously devote your energy, time, attention, and resources?

_____

_____

_____

_____

_____

_____

_____

_____

_____

5. Why do you think Jesus wanted God's "house of prayer" (Matthew 21:13; see also Isaiah 56:7) to be a place where people showed respect and reverence? What are some ways you can encourage respect and reverence in your church or worship space?

_____

_____

_____

_____

_____

_____

_____

_____

_____

_____

6. "Your body is a temple of the Holy Spirit within you," wrote St. Paul (1 Corinthians 6:19). How have you experienced Jesus "cleansing" you to make you a more fitting temple for his Spirit to dwell in?

_____

_____

_____

_____

_____

_____

_____

_____

_____

_____

Jesus: A Portrait of Zeal

Jesus, the Servant-King foretold by Zechariah, rode humbly into Jerusalem on a donkey in a spirit of peace. But in cleansing the temple, he exhibited a bold and forceful zeal for his Father's house. Jesus was moved not by a fit of temper but by righteous indignation and godly fervor.

Zeal is more than burning ardor or emotion-based enthusiasm. Rather, true zeal consists of a determined, unflagging dedication to something or to someone; a zealous spirit seeks to advance a cause, defend the truth, or render service. Godly zeal is a characteristic of great men and women of faith. David slew the Philistine aggressor, Goliath (1 Samuel 17:45-49). Deborah roused the faltering Barak into action to defeat the enemies of Israel (Judges 4:4-10). Paul first zealously persecuted those who believed in Jesus and then even more zealously proclaimed the good news of the gospel when he had become a believer (Acts 22:1-5; 2 Corinthians 11:23-27).

Just as Jesus and these heroes of the Bible spent themselves zealously for God and his service, we, too, are to be zealous for God himself, zealous for the gospel, zealous in good works, and zealous in defense of the faith.

Read and prayerfully reflect on these additional Scripture passages that describe zeal and how it is put to service for the Lord and his kingdom:

Then David said to the Philistine, "You come to me with a sword and with a spear and with a javelin; but I come to you in the name of the LORD of hosts, the God of the armies of Israel, whom you have defied. This day the LORD will deliver you into my hand. . . . And David put his hand in his bag and took out a stone, and slung it, and struck the Philistine on his forehead; the stone sank into his forehead, and he fell on his face to the ground. (1 Samuel 17:45-46, 49)

Never flag in zeal, be aglow with the Spirit, serve the Lord. (Romans 12:11)

[O]ur great God and Savior Jesus Christ . . . gave himself for us to redeem us from all iniquity and to purify for himself a people of his own who are zealous for good deeds. (Titus 2:13-14)

[W]ho is there to harm you if you are zealous for what is right? But even if you do suffer for righteousness' sake, you will be blessed. Have no fear of them, nor be troubled, but in your

hearts reverence Christ as Lord. Always be prepared to make a defense to any one who calls you to account for the hope that is in you, yet do it with gentleness and reverence.
(1 Peter 3:13-15)

[A]ccording to his promise we wait for new heavens and a new earth in which righteousness dwells. Therefore, beloved, since you wait for these, be zealous to be found by him without spot or blemish, and at peace.
(2 Peter 3:13-14)

Treasuring the Word

A Reading from *Life of Christ* by Archbishop Fulton Sheen

Entrance into Jerusalem

His last Sabbath Our Lord spent in Bethany with Lazarus and his sisters. News was now circulated that Our Lord was coming into Jerusalem. In preparation for His entrance, He sent two of His disciples into the village, where they were told they would find a colt tethered, on which no man had ridden. They were to untie it and bring it to Him.

> If anyone asks why you are untying it, Our Master needs it. *Luke 19:31*

Perhaps no greater paradox was ever written than this—on the one hand the sovereignty of the Lord, and on the other His "need." This combination of Divinity and dependence, of possession and poverty was the consequence of the Word becoming flesh. Truly, He who was rich became poor for our sakes, that we might be rich. He borrowed a boat from a fisherman from which to preach; He borrowed barley loaves and fishes from a boy to feed the multitude; He borrowed a grave from which He would rise; and now He borrowed an ass on which to enter Jerusalem. Sometimes God preempts and requisitions the things of man, as if to remind him that everything is a gift from Him. It is sufficient for those who know Him to hear: "The Lord hath need of it."

As He approached the city, a "great multitude" came to meet Him; among them were not only the citizens but also those who had come up for the feast and, of course, the Pharisees. The Roman authorities also were on the alert during great feasts lest there be an insurrection. On all previous occasions, Our Lord rejected the false enthusiasm of the people, fled the spotlight of publicity, and avoided anything that savored display. . . . But the entrance into Jerusalem was so public, that even the Pharisees said:

> All the world has gone after him. *John 12:19*

All this was in opposition to His usual manner. Before He dampened all their enthusiasm; now He kindled them. Why?

Because His "Hour" had come. It was time now for Him to make the last public affirmation of His claims. He knew it would lead to Calvary, and His Ascension and the establishment of His Kingdom on earth. Once He acknowledged their praise, then there were only two courses open to the city: confess Him as did Peter, or else crucify. Either He was their King, or else they would have no king but Caesar. No Galilean seacoast or mountaintop, but the royal city on the Passover was the best time to make His last proclamation.

He drew attention to His Kingship in two ways, first by the fulfillment of the prophecy familiar to the people, and second by the tributes of Divinity which He accepted as His own.

Matthew explicitly states that the solemn procession was to fulfill the prophecy made by Zechariah years before:

> Tell the daughter of Zion, Here is your king, who comes to you in gentleness, riding on an ass.
> *Matthew 21:5*

The prophecy came from God through a prophet, and now God Himself was bringing it to fulfillment. The prophecy of Zechariah was meant to contrast the majesty and humility of the Savior. As one looks at the ancient sculptural slabs of Assyria and Babylon, the murals of Egypt, the tombs of the Persians, and the scrolls of the Roman columns, one is stuck by the majesty of kings riding in triumph on horses or in chariots, and sometimes over the prostrate bodies of their foes. In contrast to this, here is One Who comes triumphant upon an ass. How Pilate, if he was looking out of his fortress that Sunday, must have been amused by the ridiculous spectacle of a man being proclaimed as a King, yet seated on the beast that was the symbol of the outcast—a fitting vehicle for one riding into the jaws of death. If He had entered into that city with regal pomp in the manner of conquerors, He would have given occasion to believe that He was a political Messiah. But the circumstance He chose validated His claim that His Kingdom was not of this world. There is no suggestion that the pauper King was a rival of Caesar.

The acclaim of the people was another acknowledgment of His Divinity. Many took off their garments and spread them before Him; others cut down boughs from the olive trees and palm branches and strewed them on the way. The Apocalypse speaks of a great multitude standing near the Throne of the Lamb with palms of victory in their hands. Here the palms, so often used throughout their history to signify victory, as when Simon Maccabeus entered Jerusalem, witnessed His victory—even before He was momentarily vanquished.

Then taking verses from the great Hillel which referred to the Messiah, the multitudes followed Him, shouting:

> Blessings on him who comes as king in the name of the Lord. *Luke 19:38*

Admitting now that He was the One sent by God, they practically repeated the song of the angels of Bethlehem, for the peace He brought was the reconciliation of earth and heaven. Repeated too is the salutation the Wise Men gave Him at the crib: "the King of Israel.". . .

The entry has been called triumphant; but well He knew that "Hosannas" would change to "Crucify," and palms would be turned into spears. Amid the shouts of the multitude He could hear the whispers of a Judas and the angry voices before Pilate's palace. The throne to which He was hailed was a Cross, and His real coronation would be a Crucifixion. Garments aplenty beneath His feet today, but on Friday He would be denied even His own. From the very beginning He knew what was in the heart of man, and never once did He suggest that the Redemption of men's souls could be accomplished by vocal fireworks. Though He was a King, and though they now admitted Him as their King and Lord, He knew the King's welcome which awaited Him was to be Calvary.

"Behold Your King"

Over his head they put the charge against him, which read, "This is Jesus the King of the Jews." **Matthew 27:37**

The sacred blood of Christ has quenched the flaming sword that barred access to the tree of life. The age-old night of sin has given place to the true light. **St. Leo the Great, *Sermon 15, The Passion of the Lord***

The First Station:
Jesus Is Condemned to Death

The Son of God stood bound,
bearing, too, the bonds of our sin and guilt.

Life itself stood accused, sentenced,
and condemned to death.
What irony that they thought to destroy
the one who is the source of life,
one they knew had raised men from the dead!

Jesus stood before the judgment seat.
He who has the right to judge us all
was judged himself by his own creatures—
to the shame of man,
and yet for our salvation.
How the angels must have trembled in the courts of heaven
as they looked upon this earthly court!

Sentenced to death—by whom?
Who wielded this power over God's Son?

Pilate:
lacking integrity and character,
ruled by fear and vanity,
gaming with political necessity to prevent a riot
and preserve his reputation before the eyes of Rome.

Caiaphas and the Jewish leaders:
safeguarding ritual and the status quo,
eaten by envy,
hardened in unbelief and self-righteousness,
choosing expediency to save their nation.

Me, you, all mankind:
steeped in Adam's sin.

Silently he stood,
majestic and serene, calm and composed
amid the jeering tumult and accusations roiling around him.

He had passed through the anguish of Gethsemane,
and held fast to his Father's will.
All that remained was to drink the cup to the dregs.
(Yet what human terror must have taunted his resolve
and made a knot in his stomach recoiling from the pain and horror to come.)

He was oppressed and he was afflicted,
    yet he opened not his mouth;
like a lamb that is led to the slaughter,
    and like a sheep that before its shearers is dumb,
    so he opened not his mouth.

Defenseless, ignoring the charges brought against him,
he spoke only to confirm that his kingship was not of this world.
How quick we are
to defend ourselves against the smallest wrong or imagined slight,
to protect ourselves against hurt or injury.

I have set my face like a flint,
    and I know that I shall not be put to shame;
    he who vindicates me is near.
Who will contend with me?
    Let us stand up together.
Who is my adversary?
    Let him come near to me.
Behold, the Lord GOD helps me;
    who will declare me guilty?

The word was spoken,
the judgment passed upon the Son of God:
condemned to death upon a cross.

There is therefore now no condemnation for those who are in Christ Jesus.

Matthew 26:57-68; 27:1-2, 11-31

[57]Then those who had seized Jesus led him to Caiaphas the high priest, where the scribes and the elders had gathered. [58]But Peter followed him at a distance, as far as the courtyard of the high priest, and going inside he sat with the guards to see the end. [59]Now the chief priests and the whole council sought false testimony against Jesus that they might put him to death, [60]but they found none, though many false witnesses came forward. At last two came forward [61]and said, "This fellow said, 'I am able to destroy the temple of God, and to build it in three days.'" [62]And the high priest stood up and said, "Have you no answer to make? What is it that these men testify against you?" [63]But Jesus was silent. And the high priest said to him, "I adjure you by the living God, tell us if you are the Christ, the Son of God." [64]Jesus said to him, "You have said so. But I tell you, hereafter you will see the Son of man seated at the right hand of Power, and coming on the clouds of heaven." [65]Then the high priest tore his robes, and said, "He has uttered blasphemy. Why do we still need witnesses? You have now heard his blasphemy. [66]What is your judgment?" They answered, "He deserves death." [67]Then they spat in his face, and struck him; and some slapped him, saying, "Prophesy to us, you Christ! Who is it that struck you?"

[27:1]When morning came, all the chief priests and the elders of the people took counsel against Jesus to put him to death; [2]and they bound him and led him away and delivered him to Pilate the governor.

[11]Now Jesus stood before the governor; and the governor asked him, "Are you the King of the Jews?" Jesus said to him, "You have said so." [12]But when he was accused by the chief priests and elders, he made no answer. [13]Then Pilate said to him, "Do you not hear how many things they testify against you?" [14]But he gave him no answer, not even to a single charge; so that the governor wondered greatly.

[15]Now at the feast the governor was accustomed to release for the crowd any one prisoner whom they wanted. [16]And they had then a notorious prisoner, called Barabbas. [17]So when they had gathered, Pilate said to them, "Whom do you want me to release for you, Barabbas or Jesus who is called Christ?" [18]For he knew that it was out of envy that they had delivered him up. [19]Besides, while he was sitting on the judgment seat, his wife sent word to him, "Have nothing to do with that righteous man, for I have suffered much over him today in a dream." [20]Now the chief priests and the elders persuaded the people to ask for Barabbas and destroy Jesus. [21]The governor again said to them, "Which of the two do you want me to release for you?" And they said, "Barabbas." [22]Pilate said to them, "Then what shall I do with Jesus who is called Christ?" They all said, "Let him be crucified." [23]And he said, "Why, what evil has he done?" But they shouted all the more, "Let him be crucified."

[24]So when Pilate saw that he was gaining nothing, but rather that a riot was beginning, he took water and washed his hands before the crowd, saying, "I am innocent of this righteous man's blood; see to it yourselves." [25]And all the people answered, "His blood be on us and on our children!" [26]Then he released for them Barabbas, and having scourged Jesus, delivered him to be crucified.

[27]Then the soldiers of the governor took Jesus into the praetorium, and they gathered the whole battalion before him. [28]And they stripped him and put a scarlet robe upon him, [29]and plaiting a crown of thorns they put it on his head, and put a reed in his right hand. And kneeling before him they mocked him, saying, "Hail, King of the Jews!" [30]And they spat upon him, and took the reed and struck him on the head. [31]And when they had mocked him, they stripped him of the robe, and put his own clothes on him, and led him away to crucify him.

See also Mark 14:53-65; 15:1-32; Luke 22:63–23:38

John 18:28–19:22
The Scene

[28]Then they led Jesus from the house of Caiaphas to the praetorium. It was early. They themselves did not enter the praetorium, so that they might not be defiled, but might eat the passover. [29]So Pilate went out to them and said, "What accusation do you bring against this man?" [30]They answered him, "If this man were not an evildoer, we would not have handed him over." [31]Pilate said to them, "Take him yourselves and judge him by your own law." The Jews said to him, "It is not lawful for us to put any man to death." [32]This was to fulfil the word which Jesus had spoken to show by what death he was to die.

[33]Pilate entered the praetorium again and called Jesus, and said to him, "Are you the King of the Jews?" [34]Jesus answered, "Do you say this of your own accord, or did others say it to you about me?" [35]Pilate answered, "Am I a Jew? Your own nation and the chief priests have handed you over to me; what have you done?" [36]Jesus answered, "My kingship is not of this world; if my kingship were of this world, my servants would fight, that I might not be handed over to the Jews; but my kingship is not from the world." [37]Pilate said to him, "So you are a king?" Jesus answered, "You say that I am a king. For this I was born, and for this I have come into the world, to bear witness to the truth. Every one who is of the truth hears my voice." [38]Pilate said to him, "What is truth?"

After he had said this, he went out to the Jews again, and told them, "I find no crime in him. ³⁹But you have a custom that I should release one man for you at the Passover; will you have me release for you the King of the Jews?" ⁴⁰They cried out again, "Not this man, but Barabbas!" Now Barabbas was a robber.

¹⁹:¹Then Pilate took Jesus and scourged him. ²And the soldiers plaited a crown of thorns, and put it on his head, and arrayed him in a purple robe; ³they came up to him, saying, "Hail, King of the Jews!" and struck him with their hands. ⁴Pilate went out again, and said to them, "Behold, I am bringing him out to you, that you may know that I find no crime in him." ⁵So Jesus came out, wearing the crown of thorns and the purple robe. Pilate said to them, "Here is the man!" ⁶When the chief priests and the officers saw him, they cried out, "Crucify him, crucify him!" Pilate said to them, "Take him yourselves and crucify him, for I find no crime in him." ⁷The Jews answered him, "We have a law, and by that law he ought to die, because he has made himself the Son of God." ⁸When Pilate heard these words, he was the more afraid; ⁹he entered the praetorium again and said to Jesus, "Where are you from?" But Jesus gave no answer. ¹⁰Pilate therefore said to him, "You will not speak to me? Do you not know that I have power to release you, and power to crucify you?" ¹¹Jesus answered him, "You would have no power over me unless it had been given you from above; therefore he who delivered me to you has the greater sin."

¹²Upon this Pilate sought to release him, but the Jews cried out, "If you release this man, you are not Caesar's friend; every one who makes himself a king sets himself against Caesar." ¹³When Pilate heard these words, he brought Jesus out and sat down on the judgment seat at a place called The Pavement, and in Hebrew, Gabbatha. ¹⁴Now it was the day of Preparation of the Passover; it was about the sixth hour. He said to the Jews, "Here is your King!" ¹⁵They cried out, "Away with him, away with him, crucify him!" Pilate said to them, "Shall I crucify your King?" The chief priests answered, "We have no king but Caesar." ¹⁶Then he handed him over to them to be crucified.

¹⁷So they took Jesus, and he went out, bearing his own cross, to the place called the place of a skull, which is called in Hebrew Golgotha. ¹⁸There they crucified him, and with him two others, one on either side, and Jesus between them. ¹⁹Pilate also wrote a title and put it on the cross; it read, "Jesus of Nazareth, the King of the Jews." ²⁰Many of the Jews read this title, for the place where Jesus was crucified was near the city; and it was written in Hebrew, in Latin, and in Greek. ²¹The chief priests of the Jews then said to Pilate, "Do not write, 'The King of the Jews,' but, 'This man said, I am King of the Jews.'" ²²Pilate answered, "What I have written I have written."

Reflecting on the Word

The gospel accounts of Jesus' trial before Caiaphas and the Sanhedrin, the Jewish council, record multiple false charges and the conflicting testimony that witnesses brought against him. Yet, ultimately, the crucial issue around which the trial revolved was whether this itinerant rabbi from Galilee was the long-awaited "anointed one": "Tell us if you are the Christ, the Son of God" (Matthew 26:63; see also Mark 14:61 and Luke 22:67).

Jesus had already provided abundant evidence of his identity through his words and deeds, his public proclamations and miracles. Yet the Sanhedrin refused to acknowledge the truth of this evidence and confess that Jesus is the Christ. And so the scene unfolded as Jesus broke his silence and replied to the assembly: "You have said so. But I tell you, hereafter you will see the Son of man seated at the right hand of Power, and coming on the clouds of heaven" (Matthew 26:64). With this, the chief priests and scribes accused Jesus of blasphemy and sought to put him to death (26:65-66; Mark 14:63-64). However, under Roman jurisdiction the Sanhedrin had no authority to impose capital punishment, so they referred the case to the Roman governor, Pontius Pilate (John 18:31).

Pontius Pilate was appointed governor of Judea, Idumea, and Samaria in A.D. 26. The given name "Pilate"—from the Latin *pilatus*—means a "pikeman" or one armed with a *pilum* or javelin; "Pontius" was the surname, a family name of Roman origin. Apparently Pilate was an able administrator since he remained in office ten years, while the region had gone through a total of four governors in the previous twenty years. But he was also a harsh and insensitive ruler, and was unpopular with the Jewish people. When Pilate had first marched into Jerusalem as governor, he provoked a riot by hanging a portrait of the emperor on the fortress wall across from the temple. Since Jews considered images idolatrous, they were outraged and demonstrated violently, even baring their necks to suggest that they would rather die by a sword stroke than have such an abomination overlook the temple. To avoid a massacre and Rome's disfavor, the humiliated governor backed down and removed the portrait.

As the Roman governor of the region, Pilate possessed the *jus gladii* (the right of the sword), that is, the authority to order an execution. Although the Jewish religious leaders despised Pilate, they had no other option than to submit the case against Jesus to him if they wanted Jesus to be sentenced to death. The Sanhedrin had condemned Jesus on the charge of blasphemy, but this religious accusation would mean nothing to a pagan Roman—Pilate would only be concerned with the breaking of Roman law, sedition, or treason against the empire. Hence Jesus' accusers implied that Jesus had organized a political rebellion: "We found this man perverting our nation, and forbidding us to give tribute to Caesar, and saying that he himself is Christ a king" (Luke 23:2).

Pilate balked at being used as a tool of the Jews, whom he disdained; he recognized that the chief priests were acting out of envy (Matthew 27:18) and did not readily succumb to their demands. Instead, he actively sought to thwart their desire to have Jesus executed. Perhaps Pilate also feared harming Jesus because his wife—Claudia Procula, granddaughter of the emperor Augustus—had warned him, "Have nothing to do with that righteous man, for I have suffered much over him today in a dream" (27:19).

Pilate was personally impressed with the enigmatic man he found standing so calmly without defense before him. When he asked if Jesus was aware of the charges against him, Jesus remained silent, "so that the governor wondered greatly" (Matthew 27:13-14). So Pilate put the crucial question to him outright: "Are you the King of the Jews?" (27:11; John 18:33). Jesus' reply was noncommittal, since the governor was thinking in purely political terms whereas Jesus' reign and kingship were spiritual, not material (John 18:36). Jesus answered Pilate in an idiomatic Jewish way: "You have said so" (Matthew 27:11; Luke 23:3; see also John 18:37), meaning, "The statement is yours" or "It is as you say." Jesus' answer also implied that Pilate was speaking the truth but did not know what "King of the Jews" meant. Thus, Jesus affirmed that he was a king, but in such a way that he rejected the political inferences of the phrase.

Pilate repeatedly declared Jesus innocent of any crime and tried every means he could think of to avoid condemning him—even having Jesus scourged in an attempt to appease the Jewish leaders and win the crowd's sympathy. Nonetheless, the chief priests and elders were unyielding. Ultimately, fear of damaging his career got the better of Pilate. Although he knew Jesus had done nothing deserving the death sentence, he lacked the courage and integrity to release him. He gave in, against his conscience, when the Jews reminded him that anyone who made himself a king was Caesar's rival. Moreover, Pilate knew that Rome would reprimand or remove him if there were riots again over a religious controversy. So, finally, rather than risk his position for an innocent man, he acquiesced to the chief priests' demands in order to preserve crowd control and his career (John 19:12-16).

As he handed Jesus over to be crucified, Pilate washed his hands to absolve himself of responsibility (Matthew 27:24). With this symbolic gesture, he tried to soothe his troubled conscience and evade personal accountability for his decision. Ultimately, every man and woman must, like Pilate, decide for themselves what to make of Jesus the Messiah. Each of us in a sense passes judgment on Jesus as we accept or reject him as our Lord. And it is this decision that determines the final judgment on ourselves.

The title "King of the Jews" had been suggested by the Sanhedrin when they brought Jesus before Pilate, because it had obvious political overtones. It was also used mockingly by the soldiers when they abused Jesus (Matthew 27:29). But at Jesus' birth, the gentile wise men used the title to honor the child whom the Jews failed to recognize (2:2). Now Pilate, another gentile, saw more deeply than the Jewish elders and ordered the title to be placed as the inscription on Jesus' cross (John 19:19). The crucifixion was Jesus' enthronement as King. The inscription that hung above him on the cross was written in Hebrew, the language of religion; in Latin, the language of the empire; and in Greek, the language of culture—thus serving as a universal proclamation testifying to the truth of who Jesus is. As St. Ambrose explained in his *Exposition of the Gospel of Luke,*

> The superscription is written and placed above, not below the cross, because the government is upon his shoulders [Isaiah 9:6]. What is this government if not his eternal power and Godhead? . . . The superscription is fittingly above the cross, because although the Lord Jesus was on the cross, he shines above the cross with the majesty of a king.

Jesus' death begins to make sense only when we recognize the great love that the Father has for us—so great a longing in the Father's heart for us to be restored to full friendship with him that he would ask his Son to go to such great lengths on our behalf. The words of the *Exsultet*, the proclamation sung at the Easter Vigil, marvel at God's motive: "Father, how wonderful your care for us! How boundless your merciful love! To ransom a slave you gave away your Son."

We have come full circle now from the time when Adam and Eve, by partaking of the fruit of the forbidden tree, brought sin and death into the world. Jesus Christ, the new Adam, restored our relationship with the Father through the tree of the cross. Paradoxically, it is the death of the Son of God on this tree that secured new life for us:

> How precious the gift of the cross, how splendid to contemplate! In the cross there is no mingling of good and evil, as in the tree of paradise: it is wholly beautiful to behold and good to taste. The fruit of this tree is not death but life, not darkness but light. This tree does not cast us out of paradise, but opens the way for our return. . . . This was the tree upon which the Lord, like a brave warrior wounded in hands, feet and side, healed the wounds of sin that the evil serpent had inflicted on our nature. . . . What an astonishing transformation! That death should become life, that decay should become immortality, that shame should become glory! (St. Theodore the Studite, *Oratio in adorationem crucis*)

Pondering the Word

1. Why were the Jewish elders and chief priests so determined to have Jesus sentenced to death? Which of their claims about Jesus were well founded? Which were false?

_____

_____

_____

_____

_____

_____

_____

_____

_____

_____

2. Why was Jesus silent at various points in the proceedings with the Sanhedrin (Matthew 26:63; 27:12) and Pilate (Matthew 27:14; John 19:9)? What effect did his silence have on the Jewish leaders? On Pilate?

_____

_____

_____

_____

_____

_____

_____

_____

_____

_____

3. With what adjectives or phrases would you describe Jesus' demeanor and posture before Pilate? What key declarations did Jesus make to Pilate? What does the exchange between Pilate and Jesus in John 19:10-11 indicate to you about Jesus' death?

_____

_____

_____

_____

_____

_____

_____

_____

_____

_____

4. Why do you think the chief priests were able to convince the crowd to ask that Barabbas be released (Matthew 27:15-21, 26; John 18:38-40)? What does this suggest about their influence over the people? About the people themselves?

_____

_____

_____

_____

_____

_____

_____

_____

_____

_____

5. Pilate declared several times that he found no valid charge against Jesus. Why do you think he was so convinced of Jesus' innocence? Why, in your opinion, was Pilate afraid of Jesus (Matthew 27:19; John 19:7-12)? What other fears played on him?

_____

_____

_____

_____

_____

_____

_____

_____

_____

_____

6. What contrasts between Jesus' power and worldly power are evident in the scenes of the trial and crucifixion?

_____

_____

_____

_____

_____

_____

_____

_____

_____

_____

Living the Word

1. Imagine yourself in Pilate's place. Then recall pressures or personal concerns in your life that may have allowed you to turn away from choosing God first. What might help you make better choices in the future?

_____

_____

_____

_____

_____

_____

_____

_____

_____

2. What stands out to you most strongly about Jesus' disposition toward Caiaphas and Pilate? Have you ever been slandered or falsely accused of wrongdoing? If so, how did you feel about this internally? How did you respond outwardly?

_____

_____

_____

_____

_____

_____

_____

_____

_____

3. Jesus told Pilate, "For this I was born, and for this I have come into the world, to bear witness to the truth" (John 18:37). In what ways does your own life bear witness to the truth?

_____

_____

_____

_____

_____

_____

_____

_____

_____

4. Are you facing any responsibilities or duties that you would prefer to "wash your hands" of? Why do you feel that way? Ask the Holy Spirit for help to carry or fulfill the responsibilities that weigh most heavily on you right now.

_____

_____

_____

_____

_____

_____

_____

_____

_____

5. What does the incredible price Jesus willingly paid for our salvation tell you about his love for us? About his obedience to his Father? How does it put into perspective the difficulties you have to face in your own life?

_____

_____

_____

_____

_____

_____

_____

_____

_____

6. Spend some time quietly reflecting on Christ's death, perhaps kneeling before a crucifix. Write a prayer to thank Jesus for his love and for the salvation he won for you on the cross.

_____

_____

_____

_____

_____

_____

_____

_____

_____

Rooted in the Word

Jesus: A Portrait of the Suffering Servant

John the Baptist had perceived, at least to some degree, the sacrificial nature of Jesus' life when he acknowledged him as the "Lamb of God, who takes away the sin of the world" (John 1:29). On the day of preparation, spotless lambs were made ready for sacrifice at Passover—the celebration of Israel's deliverance so many years before from slavery to the Egyptians. On that same day the Lamb of God—Jesus Christ, the Messiah—was led away to be crucified, delivering humankind once and for all from the bondage of sin and death. Like the "suffering servant" of Isaiah 53,

> He was oppressed, and he was
>   afflicted,
>   yet he opened not his mouth;
> like a lamb that is led to the
>   slaughter,
>   and like a sheep that before its
>   shearers is dumb,
>   so he opened not his mouth.
> (53:7)

Jesus' own predictions to his disciples of his sufferings and death (Matthew 16:21; 17:22-23; Mark 8:31; 9:31; Luke 9:22) and his lack of any resistance to his sentence signal his complete assent to his Father's plan of salvation that his dying would accomplish.

The "suffering servant" song—which is read during the Good Friday liturgy—ends on a triumphant note:

> [W]hen he makes himself an offering
>   for sin,
>   he shall see his offspring, he shall
>   prolong his days;
> the will of the LORD shall prosper in
>   his hand;
>   he shall see the fruit of the travail
>   of his soul and be satisfied;
> by his knowledge shall the righteous
>   one, my servant,
>   make many to be accounted
>   righteous. (Isaiah 53:10-11)

Read and prayerfully reflect on these additional Scripture passages that further describe what Jesus endured for our sake:

> I gave my back to the smiters,
>   and my cheeks to those
>   who pulled out the beard;
> I hid not my face
>   from shame and spitting.
>
> For the Lord GOD helps me;
>   therefore I have not been
>   confounded;
> therefore I have set my face like a
>   flint,
>   and I know that I shall not be put

to shame;
he who vindicates me is near.
(Isaiah 50:6-8)

[H]e had no form or comeliness that
we should look at him,
and no beauty that we should
desire him.
He was despised and rejected by men;
a man of sorrows, and acquainted
with grief;
and as one from whom men hide
their faces
he was despised, and we esteemed
him not.

Surely he has borne our griefs
and carried our sorrows;
yet we esteemed him stricken,
smitten by God, and afflicted.
But he was wounded for our
transgressions,
he was bruised for our iniquities;
upon him was the chastisement that
made us whole,
and with his stripes we are healed.

All we like sheep have gone astray;
we have turned every one to his
own way;
and the LORD has laid on him
the iniquity of us all.
(Isaiah 53:2-6)

You know that you were ransomed
from the futile ways inherited from
your fathers, not with perishable
things such as silver or gold, but with
the precious blood of Christ, like that
of a lamb without blemish or spot.
(1 Peter 1:18-19)

Christ . . . suffered for you, leaving you
an example, that you should follow in
his steps. He committed no sin; no guile
was found on his lips. When he was re-
viled, he did not revile in return; when
he suffered, he did not threaten; but he
trusted to him who judges justly. He
himself bore our sins in his body on the
tree, that we might die to sin and live to
righteousness. By his wounds you have
been healed. (1 Peter 2:21-24)

Treasuring the Word

A Reading from a Homily by Abbot John Eudes Bamberger, OCSO
Given on Good Friday, April 2, 1999, at the Abbey of the Genesee

Jesus of Nazareth, King of the Jews

Jesus of Nazareth, King of the Jews. These words even today serve as a proclamation of the true identity of the man crucified outside the walls of Jerusalem. St. John [the Evangelist] presents the passion and death of Jesus as manifesting the divine nature of our Lord, hidden to the many but revealed to his chosen faithful. The Jews understood very well that their true king was God himself. David, Solomon, and their successors were God's vicars; they did not rule in their own name—rather, they represented the rule of the Holy One of Israel. The king of Israel would appear again in history in the form of his anointed Son, the Messiah, who was to come and establish definitively the kingdom of God. The Hebrew liturgy often refers to God as king, still today, in very moving, beautifully worded prayers such as this one that is used on the Passover:

> Blessed art thou, Lord our God, King of the Universe, who createst the light of the fire . . . [and] who createst the fruit of the vine. Blessed are thou, Lord our God, King of the Universe, who has chosen and exalted us above all the nations,

and hast sanctified us with thy commandments.

These are the beliefs we must keep in mind if we would grasp what it meant that Pilate deliberately, against the objections of the Jewish rulers, had these words nailed upon the cross: Jesus of Nazareth, King of the Jews. John well appreciated the implications of this title posted above the head of the dying, rejected Jesus. For that reason he repeatedly highlights the sovereignty of Christ precisely during those episodes when he was apparently defeated. At his arrest, when having been turned over by his own religious leaders to the Roman governor, mocked and scourged he is presented to the people. And finally, when nailed to the cross where he is helpless, and is delivered over to death. The message that St. John proclaims here is that these events, far from being indications of defeat, are the enactment of God's plan of salvation. They are the revelation of the glory of God previously hidden in the man Jesus but now manifest to the eyes of faith.

The light of the resurrection was necessary for this vision of Christ as the king of God's chosen people. Today, as we reflect on the mystery of our Lord's passion and death, we are invited to follow the Evangelist in his contemplation and faith. We are given the opportunity to penetrate through the surface happenings, which are so painful to envisage and relive in some way with the Lord, to the meaning they continue to have in terms of salvation and eternity. Doing this, however, is just the beginning of the task set us by the gospel; we are to put the insights we receive from such consideration into practice in our own lives, day by day. Our task is to transform those frustrations and other sufferings, whether mental or emotional or physical, into life-giving experiences through union with the cross of Jesus.

Obviously, such transformation requires much effort but depends totally, at the same time, on the gifts of grace. We believe these graces are already won for us and will be offered to us if we but truly seek for them. If Jesus died on the cross it was, after all, for our salvation and for our sanctification. He did not hold back himself, nor did the Father spare his Son; as John tells us earlier in his gospel, it was from love for us that he gave him up to death.

"The Lord Has Risen Indeed"

Was it not necessary that the Christ should suffer these things and enter into his glory?
Luke 24:26

Amid our questions and difficulties, and even our bitter disappointments, the divine Wayfarer continues to walk at our side, opening to us the Scriptures and leading us to a deeper understanding of the mysteries of God.
Pope John Paul II, *Stay with Us, Lord*

The Road to Emmaus

The road to Emmaus:
For some
the last stretch of a long journey,
a search for the promised Savior.
Now the journey of fear and sadness and loneliness is ended
as the long-sought one reveals himself—
A new journey begins, eyes opened, hearts afire.
New life and a new day lie ahead.

The road to Emmaus:
For others
an oft-trodden road,
his strong presence a steady companion and guide
as faith is again and again challenged and deepened
with the passing from one stage of life to another.

The road to Emmaus:
For all
a journey not to be missed,
a way not to be refused,
where hearts are set afire
and blind eyes opened to truth himself.

Where do I find myself now on this road?
Where am I on this journey homeward?

At the beginning?
Dare I set out,
venturing that first step on the way that lies ahead,
mustering up courage,
gathering strength,
sure that he will walk this way with me?

Or somewhere far down the road,
in the heat of the day,
tired and weary,
looking for refreshment
and relying on his companionship
to ease the loneliness and the length of the way?

Do I stand at a crossroads,
a turning point,
a fork in the road,
with decisions to make,
choices that will determine
the direction of my life?

Or at a meeting point,
a new encounter
with my Lord and with my wayfaring companions
awaiting me at each step?

On the verge of new discovery?
Or at an impasse,
obstacles blocking my path
and forcing me to make an unexpected detour?

What must I leave behind to make this journey,
free and unburdened from my past and all my cares?

And what must I bring along?

My heart takes courage.
At every step,
at every stretch of the journey,
he walks the way beside me,
speaking words of life:

Did not our hearts burn within us
while he talked to us on the road,
while he opened to us the scriptures?

[13]That very day two of them were going to a village named Emmaus, about seven miles from Jerusalem, [14]and talking with each other about all these things that had happened. [15]While they were talking and discussing together, Jesus himself drew near and went with them. [16]But their eyes were kept from recognizing him. [17]And he said to them, "What is this conversation which you are holding with each other as you walk?" And they stood still, looking sad. [18]Then one of them, named Cleopas, answered him, "Are you the only visitor to Jerusalem who does not know the things that have happened there in these days?" [19]And he said to them, "What things?" And they said to him, "Concerning Jesus of Nazareth, who was a prophet mighty in deed and word before God and all the people, [20]and how our chief priests and rulers delivered him up to be condemned to death, and crucified him. [21]But we had hoped that he was the one to redeem Israel. Yes, and besides all this, it is now the third day since this happened. [22]Moreover, some women of our company amazed us. They were at the tomb early in the morning [23]and did not find his body; and they came back saying that they had even seen a vision of angels, who said that he was alive. [24]Some of those who were with us went to the tomb, and found it just as the women had said; but him they did not see." [25]And he said to them, "O foolish men, and slow of heart to believe all that the prophets have spoken! [26]Was it not necessary that the Christ should suffer these things and enter into his glory?" [27]And beginning with Moses and all the prophets, he interpreted to them in all the scriptures the things concerning himself.

[28]So they drew near to the village to which they were going. He appeared to be going further, [29]but they constrained him, saying, "Stay with us, for it is toward evening and the day is now far spent." So he went in to stay with them. [30]When he was at table with them, he took the bread and blessed, and broke it, and gave it to them. [31]And their eyes were opened and they recognized him; and he vanished out of their sight. [32]They said to each other, "Did not our hearts burn within us while he talked to us on the road, while he opened to us the scriptures?" [33]And they rose that same hour and returned to Jerusalem; and they found the eleven gathered together and those who were with them, [34]who said, "The Lord has risen indeed, and has appeared to Simon!" [35]Then they told what had happened on the road, and how he was known to them in the breaking of the bread.

Reflecting on the Word

Overwhelmed with anguish, two of Jesus' disciples left Jerusalem behind and set out on the way to Emmaus. Perhaps they were returning to their homes and the everyday life they had known there before they met the amazing rabbi from Galilee. Luke names only one of the two wayfarers, Cleopas.

In his *Ecclesiastical History*, Eusebius cited an early church tradition that called Cleopas the brother of Jesus' foster father, Joseph, which would have made him Jesus' uncle. Eusebius also recorded that Cleopas' son Symeon became the second bishop of Jerusalem. In light of this tradition, some scholars propose that it was Symeon who accompanied Cleopas to Emmaus. Others, citing John 19:25, suggest that Cleopas' unnamed companion may have been his wife, Mary. (The Greek of verse 25 in Luke's narrative has no gender indication and thus is literally "O foolish *ones*!"—not necessarily "men.") No matter their identities, the two had been loyal followers of Jesus and were deeply grieved by his death.

As the disciples' dreams of the Messiah and Israel's deliverance faded away, disappointment and bewilderment were all that remained. The vitality of Jesus' presence and those glorious days with him were past, and the pair gropingly sought their way toward what now seemed a dull and empty future. Then, as the two walked along discussing the events of the past days in Jerusalem, a stranger joined them and asked what they were talking about (Luke 24:15-16).

The travelers "stood still, looking sad" (Luke 24:17) and poignantly explained their grief and the pain of their unfulfilled expectations. A mighty prophet—the long-awaited "prophet like Moses" (Deuteronomy 18:15)—had been crucified. They had hoped that Jesus would be the messianic deliverer of Israel and the one to establish a new order. But with his death, their hopes had been dashed. Moreover, some of their friends had told the strange story that when they visited his tomb, Jesus' body was missing and a vision of angels had declared that he was alive (Luke 24:19-24)! All this was too much for their dazed, sorrowing minds to grasp.

But Jesus did not leave the disciples to stand paralyzed by pain and numbed by disillusionment. First he chastised them for being "slow of heart to believe all that the prophets have spoken!" (Luke 24:25). Then he opened their minds to the true meaning of the Scriptures concerning himself, with an explanation that progressed step-by-step as if paralleling their journey along the road.

"Was it not necessary that the Messiah should suffer these things and so enter into his glory?" Jesus asked (Luke 24:26). The key to understanding Jesus' messianic identity and his mission is found in this verse. With these words, Jesus corrected the disciples' mistaken notion of an earthly and political messiah and showed them the "super"-natural nature of his mission—to save and restore humankind to union with the Father.

"[B]eginning with Moses and all the prophets, he interpreted to them in all the scriptures the things concerning himself" (24:27). The Greek form of "all the prophets" implies that Jesus touched on each and every one of the ancient prophecies regarding the Messiah as he gave the two travelers an overview of salvation history. With his explanation, he demonstrated how his entire life—his birth, ministry, death, and resurrection—was preordained in Scripture.

Later Jesus would repeat this Scripture lesson to the eleven when he appeared to them in his resurrected body: "'[E]verything written about me in the law of Moses and the prophets and the psalms must be fulfilled.' Then he opened their minds to understand the scriptures, and said to them, 'Thus it is written, that the Christ should suffer and on the third day rise from the dead.'" (Luke 24:44-46). From its earliest days the Christian church recognized the significance of Christ's fulfillment of prophecy; its faith in Jesus the Messiah was rooted in God's word. As St. Paul attested, "I delivered to you as of first importance what I also received, that Christ died for our sins in accordance with the scriptures, that he was buried, that he was raised on the third day in accordance with the scriptures" (1 Corinthians 15:3-4).

It was almost evening as Cleopas and his companion drew near to Emmaus. Comforted and encouraged by the stranger's words, they begged him to stay with them as their guest (Luke 24:28-29). St. Gregory Nazianzen, one of the Eastern Fathers of the Church, compared the experience of the two disciples with our own:

The journey ends when they reach the village. The two disciples who, without realizing it, have been deeply stirred by the words and love shown by God made man, are sorry to see him leaving. For Jesus "appeared to be going further." This Lord of ours never forces himself on us. He wants us to turn to him freely, when we begin to grasp the purity of his Love which he has placed in our souls. We have to hold him back ("they constrained him") and beg him: "Stay with us, for it is towards evening, and the day is now far spent."

That's just like us—always short on daring, perhaps because we are insincere, or because we feel embarrassed. Deep down, what we are really thinking is: "Stay with us, because our souls are shrouded in darkness and You alone are the light. You alone can satisfy this longing that consumes us." For we know full well which among all things fair and honorable is the best—to possess God for ever. (*Epistuale*, 212)

We hear echoes of "Stay with us"—which also means "abide"—in Jesus' words to his disciples in the Gospel of John (15:4-10): "Abide in me, and I in you." The allusion to the lateness of the hour—"it is toward evening and the day is now far spent" (Luke 24:29)—highlights the contrast between light and darkness. It is a theme used frequently by the Evangelist John (John 1:5; 8:12; 12:35) and by St. Paul (2 Corinthians 4:6; 6:14; Ephesians 5:8; 1 Thessalonians 5:4-5).

"[W]hen he was at table with them, he took the bread and blessed, and broke it, and gave it to them" (Luke 24:30). This same sequence of actions is described in the accounts of the multiplication of the loaves (Luke 9:16), the Last Supper (Matthew 26:26; Luke 22:19), and the early church's celebration of the eucharistic liturgy (Acts 2:42; 20:7). As the weary disciples reclined together at table in Emmaus, they encountered Christ in a spiritual way: They discerned his presence in the meal after their hearts had been prepared by his word.

The structure of the Emmaus episode reflects the structure of the eucharistic liturgy, where Jesus gives himself to the church first in word and then in sacrament, first in the proclamation of Scripture and then in Communion, the bread of life. Indeed, it is through these actions of the risen Lord—the interpretation of Scripture and the breaking of the bread—that he remains present with us and with the church.

With the breaking of the bread, "their eyes were opened [*dianoigo*] and they recognized him" (Luke 24:31). The Greek verb *dianoigo*—"to open up completely"—is used seven times by Luke in his gospel and in the Acts of the Apostles to describe a metaphorical or spiritual opening of the eyes or of the mind and heart and a deeper understanding or revelation. As St. Leo the Great so eloquently noted, "Their eyes were opened in the breaking of bread, opened far more happily to the sight of their own glorified humanity than were the eyes of our first parents to the shame of their sin."

Upon recognizing Jesus, Cleopas and his companion shook off their weariness and hastened back to Jerusalem, their hearts burning with new understanding and hope (Luke 24:32-35). What a contrast, then, between their sad walk to Emmaus and their joyful, hurried return to the holy city to share their discovery with their friends! Centuries later their story is still being told and the good news passed on: "The Lord has risen indeed!" (24:34).

The Emmaus story is unique to Luke's gospel. Interestingly, a pattern similar to that of the Emmaus narrative is to be seen in Luke's account of the baptism of the Ethiopian official by Philip in the Acts of the Apostles (8:26-40). Both include a journey; an ignorance of Scripture; the interpretation of Scripture, with the emphasis that Jesus must suffer; an insistence to stay; a significant (sacramental) action; and a sudden and mysterious disappearance. How often our own personal journey to an encounter with the risen Lord reflects these same elements!

Finally, as Pope John Paul II reminded those gathered at an audience with him,

> However tiring, the road to Emmaus leads from a sense of discouragement and bewilderment to the fullness of Easter faith. In retracing this journey, we too are joined by the mysterious traveling Companion. Jesus approaches us on the road, meeting us where we are and asking us the essential questions that open the heart to hope. He has many things to explain about his and our destiny. In particular, he reveals that every human life must pass through his Cross to enter into glory. But Christ does something more: he breaks the bread of sharing for us, offering that Eucharistic Table in which the Scriptures acquire their full meaning and reveal the unique and shining features of the Redeemer's face.

Pondering the Word

1. What do their conversation and behavior at the beginning of the story indicate about Cleopas and his companion? What do their actions at the end of the story add to your picture of them?

_____

_____

_____

_____

_____

_____

_____

_____

_____

_____

2. What did the travelers already believe about Jesus before he joined them on the road? What mistaken ideas did they hold about him?

_____

_____

_____

_____

_____

_____

_____

_____

_____

_____

3. What, in your opinion, may be reasons why Cleopas and his companion failed to recognize Jesus (Luke 24:16) and were "slow of heart to believe" (24:25)? Do you think their attitude was reasonable? What other characters in the gospels also failed to recognize Jesus? On the other hand, whom did Jesus commend for their faith and belief in him?

_____

_____

_____

_____

_____

_____

_____

_____

_____

_____

4. Note the key points of Jesus' contact with the disciples as Luke's narrative unfolds. What does Jesus' way of approaching the two and interacting with them reveal about him? What might be the significance of Jesus "vanishing from their sight" (Luke 24:31) once the disciples recognized him?

_____

_____

_____

_____

_____

_____

_____

_____

_____

_____

5. How does the Emmaus story illustrate the importance of Scripture? What does it suggest about the relationship between God's word and faith?

_____

_____

_____

_____

_____

_____

_____

_____

_____

_____

6. Why do you think Jesus explained the Scriptures to the disciples before the meal instead of after it? What might be the significance of the disciples' eyes being "opened" (Luke 24:31) after Jesus took the bread, blessed it, broke it, and gave it to them?

_____

_____

_____

_____

_____

_____

_____

_____

_____

_____

Living the Word

1. Have you ever felt like these two disciples, downcast and disappointed or without hope for your future? When? What were your "prayer conversations" with Jesus like then? What particular words of the Lord have comforted or encouraged you in difficult times?

_____

_____

_____

_____

_____

_____

_____

_____

_____

_____

2. What could "blind" you from recognizing God's presence in your daily life? Your preconceived ideas? Pain? Busyness? How might your eyes be opened?

_____

_____

_____

_____

_____

_____

_____

_____

_____

_____

3. What is the basis of your faith in Jesus' resurrection? How does Jesus' resurrection affect your daily life? Your outlook for the future?

_____

_____

_____

_____

_____

_____

_____

_____

_____

4. How has your study of the Old Testament prophets enhanced your personal relationship with Jesus the Messiah? What might you do to continue to deepen your encounters with Jesus through Scripture and increase your understanding of God's word?

_____

_____

_____

_____

_____

_____

_____

_____

_____

5. How has the account of the meal in Emmaus (Luke 24:30-31) deepened your understanding and appreciation of the Eucharist? What might you do to express your love for Christ present in the Eucharist?

_____

_____

_____

_____

_____

_____

_____

_____

_____

6. What aspect of the Emmaus story do you find most meaningful for you at this time in your life? Why? Have you ever had any experience similar to the Emmaus episode or that of the Ethiopian official (Acts 8:26-40)? What impact did this have on you?

_____

_____

_____

_____

_____

_____

_____

_____

_____

Jesus: A Portrait of the Risen Lord

When Cleopas and his companion had returned to Jerusalem and were sharing their good news with the disciples who were gathered together there, Jesus suddenly stood among them. In this scene and various other post-resurrection scenes recorded by the Evangelists, the men and women who had known Jesus well before his crucifixion responded with incredulity, fear, doubt, or wonderment. Clearly Jesus' appearance looked altered—to some, even unrecognizable; his body had in some definite way been transformed by the resurrection.

Jesus ate in the presence of his followers several times to assure them that he was not a ghost or insubstantial vision (Luke 24:41-43; John 21:9-13; Acts 10:40-41). He invited the apostles to "handle" him and showed them the wounds in his hands and feet and side (Luke 24:39-40; John 20:27) to verify that his risen body was the same body that had been crucified. Indeed, he still had flesh and bones (Luke 24:39). "Yet at the same time," explains the *Catechism of the Catholic Church*, "this authentic, real body possesses the new properties of a glorious body: not limited by space and time but able to be present how and when he wills; for Christ's humanity can no longer be confined to earth and belongs henceforth only to the Father's divine realm" (645).

Jarius' daughter, the young man of Nain, and Lazarus, the brother of Martha and Mary, had been raised by Jesus from the dead, but they returned to ordinary earthly life and would die again. Christ's own resurrection after his death on the cross was radically different: "In his risen body he passes from the state of death to another life beyond time and space. . . . He shares the divine life in his glorious state" (CCC, 646).

In the creed, we profess our faith in Jesus' resurrection and "in the resurrection of the body"—that is, in our own future resurrection. How our bodies of flesh will be transformed into spiritual bodies "exceeds our imagination and understanding; it is accessible only to faith" (CCC, 1000). Yet we know that "the dead will be raised imperishable, and we shall be changed. . . . When the perishable puts on the imperishable, and the mortal puts on immortality, then shall come to pass the saying that is written: 'Death is swallowed up in victory'" (1 Corinthians 15:52, 54).

Read and prayerfully reflect on these additional Scripture passages that attest to Jesus' resurrection and also describe the resurrection that we eagerly await:

[T]he souls of the righteous are in the
hand of God,

and no torment will ever touch them.
In the eyes of the foolish they seemed
    to have died,
and their departure was thought to be
    an affliction,
and their going from us to be their
    destruction;
but they are at peace.
For though in the sight of men they
    were punished,
their hope is full of immortality.
Having been disciplined a little, they
    will receive great good,
because God tested them and found
    them worthy of himself;
like gold in the furnace he tried them,
and like a sacrificial burnt offering
    he accepted them.
In the time of their visitation they will
    shine forth,
and will run like sparks through the
    stubble.
They will govern nations and rule
    over peoples,
and the Lord will reign over them for
    ever.
Those who trust in him will
    understand truth,
and the faithful will abide with him
    in love,
because grace and mercy are upon his
    elect,
and he watches over his holy ones.
(Wisdom 3:1-9)

The doors were shut, but Jesus came and stood among [the disciples], and said, "Peace be with you." Then he said to Thomas, "Put your finger here, and see my hands; and put out your hand, and place it in my side; do not be faithless, but believing." Thomas answered him, "My Lord and my God!" Jesus said to him, "Have you believed because you have seen me? Blessed are those who have not seen and yet believe." (John 20:26-29)

[Peter said to Cornelius:] "[W]e are witnesses to all that [Jesus] did both in the country of the Jews and in Jerusalem. They put him to death by hanging him on a tree; but God raised him on the third day and made him manifest; not to all the people but to us who were chosen by God as witnesses, who ate and drank with him after he rose from the dead. And he commanded us to preach to the people, and to testify that he is the one ordained by God to be judge of the living and the dead." (Acts 10:39-42)

What is sown is perishable, what is raised is imperishable. It is sown in dishonor, it is raised in glory. It is sown in weakness, it is raised in power. It is sown a physical body, it is raised a spiritual body. If there is a physical body, there is also a spiritual body. Thus it is written,

"The first man Adam became a living being"; the last Adam became a life-giving spirit. But it is not the spiritual which is first but the physical, and then the spiritual. The first man was from the earth, a man of dust; the second man is from heaven. As was the man of dust, so are those who are of the dust; and as is the man of heaven, so are those who are of heaven. Just as we have borne the image of the man of dust, we shall also bear the image of the man of heaven. I tell you this, brethren: flesh and blood cannot inherit the kingdom of God, nor does the perishable inherit the imperishable. (1 Corinthians 15:42-50)

[W]e would not have you ignorant, brethren, concerning those who are asleep, that you may not grieve as others do who have no hope. For since we believe that Jesus died and rose again, even so, through Jesus, God will bring with him those who have fallen asleep. For this we declare to you by the word of the Lord, that we who are alive, who are left until the coming of the Lord, shall not precede those who have fallen asleep. For the Lord himself will descend from heaven with a cry of command, with the archangel's call, and with the sound of the trumpet of God. And the dead in Christ will rise first; then we who are alive, who are left, shall be caught up together with them in the clouds to meet the Lord in the air; and so we shall always be with the Lord. Therefore comfort one another with these words. (1 Thessalonians 4:13-18)

Treasuring the Word

A Reading from a Message by Pope John Paul II
Given on Good Friday, April 21, 2000, at the Colosseum in Rome

When Jesus Draws Near

"Was it not necessary that the Christ should suffer these things and enter into his glory?" (Luke 24:26).

These words of Jesus to the two disciples on their way to Emmaus echo deep within us this evening, at the end of the Way of the Cross at the Colosseum. Like us, they had heard talk of the events surrounding the passion and crucifixion of Jesus. On the way back to their village, Christ draws near as an unknown pilgrim, and they hasten to tell him everything "about Jesus, . . . who was a prophet mighty in deed and word before God and all the people" (Luke 24:19), and how the chief priests and rulers delivered him up to be condemned to death and how he was crucified (24:20-21). And they conclude sadly: "But we had hoped that he was the one to redeem Israel. Yes, and besides all this, it is now the third day since this happened" (24:21).

"We had hoped. . . ." The disciples are discouraged and dejected. For us too it is difficult to understand why the way of salvation should pass through suffering and death.

"Was it not necessary that the Christ should suffer these things and enter into his glory?" (Luke 24:26). Let us too ask this question at the end of the traditional Stations of the Cross at the Colosseum.

Soon, from this place sanctified by the blood of the first martyrs, we shall go away, each on our own way. We shall return home, turning over in our minds the very same events which the disciples of Emmaus were discussing.

May Jesus draw near to each one of us; may he become for us too a companion on the road! As he walks with us, he will explain that it was for our sake that he went to Calvary, for us that he died, in fulfillment of the Scriptures. Thus the sorrowful event of the crucifixion, which we have just meditated upon, will become for each of us an eloquent lesson.

Dear Brothers and Sisters! The people of today need to meet Christ crucified and risen!

Who, if not the condemned Savior, can fully understand the pain of those unjustly condemned?

Who, if not the King scorned and humiliated, can meet the expectations of the countless men and women who live without hope or dignity?

Who, if not the crucified Son of God, can know the sorrow and loneliness of so many lives shattered and without a future?

The French poet Paul Claudel wrote that the Son of God "has shown us the way out of suffering and the possibility of its transformation" (*Positions et propositions*). Let us open our hearts to Christ: He himself will respond to our deepest yearnings. He himself will unveil for us the mysteries of his passion and death on the cross.

"Then their eyes were opened and they recognized him" (Luke 24:31). As Jesus speaks, the hearts of the two disconsolate travelers find a new serenity and begin to burn with joy. They recognize the Master in the breaking of bread.

Like them, may the people of today be able to recognize in the breaking of bread, in the mystery of the Eucharist, the presence of their Savior. May they encounter him in the Sacrament of his Passover, and welcome him as their fellow traveler along the way. He will listen to them and bring them comfort. He will become their guide, leading them along the paths of life towards the Father's house.

We adore you, O Christ, and we bless you, because by your holy cross, you have redeemed the world!

Source Notes and Acknowledgments

This section indicates the sources of material quoted in *God's Promises Fulfilled: A Scriptural Journey with Jesus the Messiah.*

Reflection 1: Paradise Lost

Page 8:
Francis Martin, *The Fire in the Cloud: Lenten Meditations* (Ann Arbor, MI: Servant Publications, 2001), 33.

Page 11:
Sister Mary Francis, *A Right to Be Merry* (New York: Sheed & Ward, 1956), 99–100.

Page 12:
Baron Gottfried van Swieten, English libretto for Franz Joseph Haydn's oratorio *The Creation*, www.geocities.com/thedarkrequiem/bvscreation.html.

Page 13:
Irenaeus, *Against Heresies*, quoted in *The Liturgy of the Hours, Volume I* (New York: Catholic Book Publishing Co., 1975), 244.

Exsultet, quoted in *The Liturgy of Holy Week* (Collegeville, MN: The Liturgical Press, 1991), 106.

Page 20:
Centred on Love: The Poems of St. John of the Cross, trans. Marjorie Flower, OCD (Varroville, Australia: The Carmelite Nuns), 55. Reprinted with permission of the Varroville Carmel.

Pages 22–23:
The Lenten Triodion, translated from the original Greek by Mother Mary and Archimandrite Kallistos Ware (South Canaan, PA: St. Tikhon's Seminary Press, 2002), 168–170. Copyright © 1977,

Mother Mary, of the Monastery of the Veil of the Mother of God, Bussy-en-Othe, and Archimandrite Kallistos Timothy Ware. Reprinted with permission of Kallistos Ware.

Reflection 2: The House of David

Page 24:
Bernard of Clairvaux, *On the Christian Year: Selections from His Sermons*, trans. a Religious of CSMV (London: A.R. Mowbray & Co. Limited), 14.

Page 29:
Damasus Winzen, *Pathways in Scripture* (Ann Arbor, MI: Servant Books, 1976), 123.

Page 30:
Jerusalem Catecheses, quoted in *The Liturgy of the Hours, Volume II* (New York: Catholic Book Publishing Co., 1976), 609.

Pages 39–40:
Damasus Winzen, *Pathways in Scripture* (Ann Arbor, MI: Servant Books, 1976), 114–116, 124. Copyright © 1976 by Servant Books. Reprinted with permission of St. Anthony Messenger Press.

Reflection 3: Isaiah's Oracles of Hope

Page 42:
Advent Antiphon, quoted in *The Liturgy of the Hours, Volume I* (New York: Catholic Book Publishing Co., 1975), 342.

Page 55:
Athanasius, *Oratio 1 contra Arianos* 47, quoted in Raniero Cantalamessa, *The Holy Spirit in the Life of Jesus* (Collegeville, MN: The Liturgical Press, 1994), 12.

Pages 57–58:
John Paul II, *Theotókos: Woman, Mother, Disciple: A Catechesis on Mary, Mother of God, Volume Five* (Boston: Pauline Books & Media, 2000), 64–67. Given at a general audience on 31 January 1996. Reprinted with permission of Libreria Editrice Vaticana.

Reflection 4: "You Shall Call His Name Jesus"

Page 60:
Père Jacques (Lucien-Louis Bunel), quoted in Francis J. Murphy, *Père Jacques: Resplendent in Victory* (Washington, DC: ICS Publications, 1998), 155–156.

Page 65:
John Henry Newman, *Parochial and Plain Sermons, Volume 2* (San Francisco: Ignatius Press, 1987), 307.

John Paul II, *Guardian of the Redeemer, no. 3*, quoted in Francis Fernandez, *In Conversation with God—Volume Six* (London: Scepter Ltd., 1997), 138.

Page 66:
Oscar Romero, *The Violence of Love*, trans. James R. Brockman (Farmington, PA: The Plough Publishing House, 1998), 113.

Page 74:
Theodotus of Ancyra, "On the Day of the Lord's Nativity," quoted in Aidan Nichols, *Epiphany: A Theological Introduction to Catholicism* (Collegeville, MN: The Liturgical Press, 1996), 119.

Pages 76–77:
Maria Boulding, *The Coming of God* (Conception, MO: The Printery House, 2000), 24–26. Copyright © 1982, 1994, 2000 by Maria Boulding. Reprinted with permission of The Printery House.

Reflection 5: Herald of the Messiah

Page 78:
John Eudes Bamberger, OCSO, Homily on Feast of St. John of the Cross, 14 December 2000, www.abbotjohneudes.org/h14dec00.html.

Page 83:
Jerome, *Epist. 125, 7 (ad Rusticum)*, quoted in André Retif, *John the Baptist: Missionary of Christ* (Westminster, MD: The Newman Press, 1953), 24.

Josephus, *Antiquities* 18.5.2 116–119. http://homepages.which.net/~radical.faith/background/josephus2.htm.

Page 84:
André Retif, *John the Baptist: Missionary of Christ* (Westminster, MD: The Newman Press, 1953), 103.

Page 91:
Augustine, *Sermon 293, 3*, quoted in *The Liturgy of the Hours, Volume I* (New York: Catholic Book Publishing Co., 1975), 261.

John of the Cross, *The Ascent of Mount Carmel*, Book 2, Chapter 22, quoted in *The Liturgy of the Hours, Volume I* (New York: Catholic Book Publishing Co., 1975), 212.

Pages 93–94:
François Mauriac, *Life of Jesus*, trans. Julie Kernan (New York: David McKay Company, Inc., 1951), 17–20. Copyright © 1937 by Julie Kernan. Used with permission of McKay, a division of Random House, Inc.

Reflection 6: The Good News of the Kingdom

Page 96:
Erasmo Leiva-Merikakis, *Fire of Mercy, Heart of the Word: Meditations on the Gospel according to Saint Matthew, Volume One* (San Francisco: Ignatius Press, 1996), 170.

Page 100:
Oscar Romero, *The Violence of Love*, trans. James R. Brockman (Farmington, PA: The Plough Publishing House, 1998), 31–32.

Erasmo Leiva-Merikakis, *Fire of Mercy, Heart of the Word: Meditations on the Gospel according to Saint Matthew, Volume One* (San Francisco: Ignatius Press, 1996), 158.

Page 102:
John Paul II, *Rich in Mercy*, 30 November 1980, no. 3, www.vatican.va/edocs/ENG0215/__P4.HTM.

Page 109:
John Paul II, *Rich in Mercy*, 30 November 1980, no. 3, www.vatican.va/edocs/ENG0215/__P4.HTM.

Pages 111–112:
Romano Guardini, *The Inner Life of Jesus*, 47, 49-52. Copyright © 1959. Published by Regnery Publishing, Inc. All rights reserved. Reprinted by special permission of Regnery Publishing, Inc., Washington, DC.

Reflection 7: Flashes of Glory

Page 114:
Byzantine Hymn for the Feast of the Transfiguration, quoted in Brother Victor-Antoine d'Avila-Latourrette, *Blessings of the Daily: A Monastic Book of Days* (Liguori, MO: Liguori/Triumph, 2002), 302.

Page 117:
Alfred MacBride, *The Kingdom and the Glory: Meditation and Commentary on the Gospel of Matthew* (Huntington, IN: Our Sunday Visitor Publishing Division, Our Sunday Visitor, Inc., 1992), 100.

Page 118:
Maria Boulding, *The Coming of God* (Conception, MO: The Printery House, 2000), 132.

Leo the Great, *Sermon 51, 3-4. 8*, quoted in *The Liturgy of the Hours, Volume II* (New York: Catholic Book Publishing Co., 1976), 149.

Page 119:
Louise Perrotta, *2004: A Book of Grace-Filled Days* (Chicago: Loyola Press, 2003), 252.

Page 120:
John Paul II, *On the Most Holy Rosary*, 16 October 2002, no. 9, www.vatican.va/holy_father/john_paul_ii/apost_letters/documents/hf_jp-ii_apl_20021016_rosarium-virginis-mariae_en.html.

Page 127:
Fulton J. Sheen, *Life of Christ* (New York: Image Books/ Doubleday, 1990), 158.

Pages 129-131:
Karl Rahner, *The Great Church Year: The Best of Karl Rahner's Homilies, Sermons, and Meditations*, ed. Albert Raffelt, translation ed. Harvey D. Egan (New York: The Crossroad Publishing Company, 1993), 340-342. English translation copyright © 1993 by The Crossroad Publishing Company. Reprinted by permission of The Crossroad Publishing Company.

Reflection 8: "Hosanna to the Son of David!"

Page 135:
Andrew of Crete, *Oratio 9 in ramos pamarum*, quoted in *The Liturgy of the Hours, Volume II* (New York: Catholic Book Publishing Co., 1976), 419–420.

Page 136:
The Navarre Bible: The Gospel of Saint Luke, with a commentary by the members of the Faculty of Theology of the University of Navarre (Blackrock, Ireland: Four Courts Press, 1993), 213.

Pages 147–149:
Fulton J. Sheen, *Life of Christ* (New York: Image Books/ Doubleday, 1990), 260–263. Copyright © 1958, 1977 by Fulton J. Sheen. Reprinted with permission of Doubleday, a division of Random House, Inc.

Reflection 9: "Behold Your King"

Page 150:
Leo the Great, *Sermon 15, The Passion of the Lord*, 3–4, quoted in *The Liturgy of the Hours, Volume II* (New York: Catholic Book Publishing Co., 1976), 313.

Page 158:
Ambrose, *Exposition of the Gospel of Luke 10.112–13*, quoted in *Ancient Christian Commentary on Scripture: Luke*, ed. Arthur A. Just, Jr. (Downers Grove, IL: InterVarsity Press, 2003), 363.

Exsultet, quoted in *The Liturgy of Holy Week* (Collegeville, MN: The Liturgical Press, 1991), 106.

Theodore the Studite, *Oratio in adorationem crucis*, quoted in *The Liturgy of the Hours, Volume II* (New York: Catholic Book Publishing Co., 1976), 677–678.

Pages 167–168:
John Eudes Bamberger, OCSO, "Jesus of Nazareth, King of the Jews." Homily given on Good Friday, 2 April 1999. Copyright © Abbey of the Genesee. www.abbotjohneudes.org/h2apr99.html. Reprinted with permission of the author.

Reflection 10: "The Lord Has Risen Indeed"

Page 170:
John Paul II, *Stay with Us, Lord*, Apostolic Letter for the Year of the Eucharist, 7 October 2004, no. 1, www.vatican.va/holy_father/john_paul_ii/apost_letters/documents/hf_jp-ii_apl_20041008_mane-nobiscum-domine_en.html.

Page 174:
Eusebius, *Ecclesiastical History*, Book III, Chapter 11, www.newadvent.org/fathers/250103.htm.

Page 175:
Gregory Nazianzen, *Epistuale, 212*, quoted in *The Navarre Bible: The Gospel of Saint Luke*, with a commentary by the members of the Faculty of Theology of the University of Navarre (Blackrock, Ireland: Four Courts Press, 1993), 263.

Page 176:
Leo the Great, *Sermo 1 de Ascensione*, 2–4, quoted in *The Liturgy of the Hours, Volume II* (New York: Catholic Book Publishing Co., 1976), 898–899.

Page 177:
John Paul II, General Audience, 18 April 2001, www.catholic-forum.com/saints/pope0264ql.htm.

Pages 187–188:
John Paul II, Message given on Good Friday, 21 April 2000, www.catholic-forum.com/saints/pope0264ad.htm. Reprinted with permission of Libreria Editrice Vaticana.

Also in the Scriptural Journey Series

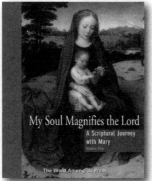

My Soul Magnifies the Lord
A Scriptural Journey with Mary
by Jeanne Kun

Follow in the footsteps of the first disciple of Jesus—his mother Mary. This unique book focuses on ten important gospel scenes in the life of the Blessed Virgin Mary, from her *fiat* at the annunciation to her presence in the upper room at Pentecost. 184 pages, 7⅜ x 9, softcover, $12.95
Item# BIGVE3

"By presenting the milestones of Mary's life as recorded in the Bible, this Scripture study can do a great deal to increase its readers' faith and humbleness of heart."
National Catholic Register

"An enticing aid to prayer."
Bible Today

My Lord and My God!
A Scriptural Journey with the Followers of Jesus
by Jeanne Kun

Jesus deeply touched the lives of those who became his disciples, followers, and friends. *My Lord and My God! A Scriptural Journey with the Followers of Jesus* is based on ten gospel characters who encountered Jesus in a life-changing way. Simon Peter, Bartimaeus, Mary of Bethany, Joseph of Arimathea, Thomas—and others—show just how diverse the faces of discipleship are. This book is suitable for small-group discussion or individual use. 192 pages, 7⅜ x 9, softcover, $12.95
Item# BDSCE5

"Once again I'm inspired by a work from Jeanne Kun. She has a gift, born from her own experience of the ways of God, to assist us in encountering Christ. In her latest book, *My Lord and My God! A Scriptural Journey with the Followers of Jesus,* biblical figures come to life, and we meet the Lord Jesus Christ with them."
> Fr. Jeffrey Huard, Director of Campus Ministry
> University of St. Thomas
> St. Paul, Minnesota

To order call 1-800-775-9673 or order online at www.wordamongus.org